THE GREAT CHICAGO FIRE

In Eyewitness Accounts and 70 Contemporary Photographs and Illustrations

Compiled and edited with an
introduction by DAVID LOWE

DOVER PUBLICATIONS, INC.
NEW YORK

for
MURIEL MORRIS GARDINER BUTTINGER

ALSO BY DAVID LOWE

Lost Chicago
Thirty-Two Picture Postcards of Old Boston
Thirty-Two Picture Postcards of Old Chicago
Thirty-Two Picture Postcards of Old London
New York, N.Y.
Views of a Splendid World

Frontispiece: Flames appear to create a "rain of fire" at the Chamber of Commerce, which stood on the southeast corner of Washington and La Salle Streets. (*Harper's Weekly,* October 28, 1871)

Copyright © 1979 by Dover Publications, Inc.
All rights reserved under Pan American and International Copyright Conventions.

Published in Canada by General Publishing Company, Ltd., 30 Lesmill Road, Don Mills, Toronto, Ontario.
Published in the United Kingdom by Constable and Company, Ltd., 10 Orange Street, London WC2H 7EG.

This Dover edition, first published in 1979, is an unabridged republication of the eyewitness accounts as published in *Reminiscences of Chicago During the Great Fire,* The Lakeside Press, R. R. Donnelley & Sons Company, Chicago, 1915. The Publisher's Preface and Introduction of that edition are here omitted. For this Dover edition a new Introduction has been written by David Lowe, who has also selected the illustrations and prepared captions.

Book design by Carol Belanger Grafton

International Standard Book Number: 0-486-23771-0
Library of Congress Catalog Card Number: 78-73518

Manufactured in the United States of America
Dover Publications, Inc.
180 Varick Street
New York, N.Y. 10014

Acknowledgments

The curious combination of terror and wonder inspired by the Great Chicago Fire of 1871 is captured with striking immediacy in these memoirs of men and women who lived through that famous holocaust. Their recollections appeared in various places in the years after the fire, including the second volume, published in 1885, of Alfred T. Andreas' monumental three-volume *History of Chicago*. In 1915, under the editorship of Mabel McIlvaine, the essays were published in the Lakeside Classics series issued by The Lakeside Press of Chicago under the title *Reminiscences of Chicago During the Great Fire*. They are here reissued with, for the first time, illustrations drawn from the archives of the Chicago Historical Society and from the leading periodicals of the day such as *Harper's* and *Leslie's* weeklies.

I would like to thank all of those who helped me when I was at work on this volume. At the head of any list of acknowledgments must be the Chicago Historical Society and its director, Harold K. Skramstad, Jr. I would also like to thank the staff of the Society's Graphics Department, especially Julia Westerberg and Miriam Blazowski. Much of my knowledge of the Great Chicago Fire was gained while doing research at the Newberry Library. It would be impossible to name all of those to whom I am indebted there, but I do wish to mention Lawrence W. Towner, president of the Newberry Library; James M. Wells, vice-president; and Richard H. Brown, director of research and education. In New York my research was carried out at the New York Public Library. I would like to acknowledge my obligation to that institution for the use of the Frederick Lewis Allen Room and to express my thanks to the staff of the Local History and Genealogy Room: Gunther Pohl, Timothy Beard, Natalie Seweryn and Frank Bradley.

D. L.

Contents

Introduction

The nineteenth century was a time of great metropolitan fires, when almost every major American city came close to burning down; New York in 1835; Charleston, South Carolina, in 1838; Pittsburgh in 1845; Philadelphia in 1865; Portland, Maine, in 1866; Boston in 1872. But no fire caught the nation's imagination as did the fire which broke out in Chicago shortly after 9:00 o'clock on Sunday evening, October 8, 1871. It was the San Francisco earthquake of urban fires. No other American city dates its history as before or after "The Fire" the way Chicago does. No other city commemorates its conflagration on its flag or has as its most famous monument a structure revered because it survived the flames. The Fire was indeed Chicago's great divide, the B.C. and A.D. of the city.

Chicago in the autumn of 1871 was, in every sense of the word, a boom town [Plate 1]. Wheat and corn, cattle and hogs, railroads and farm machinery, lumber and shoes and a dozen other industries had made it the fastest-growing city in the United States. It boasted more than 334,000 people and its 59,500 structures, spread over 23,000 acres, were valued at some $620 million. Its construction reflected a boom-town mentality. Speed was the name of the game. Not that Chicago was, as some writers have said, a wooden shantytown. The hotels and banks and office blocks and theaters and department stores of its commerical center and many of the homes of its prosperous classes were constructed of brick, stone and iron. But just a month before the fire, the *Chicago Tribune* had complained in an editorial of the shabby construction of some of the city's most pretentious buildings. The newspaper warned that Chicago's brick buildings were often only one brick thick, so that their facades were constantly falling into the street, and that the cornices of its stone buildings were so flimsy that they often came crashing down on the heads of pedestrians. As for the city's cast-iron structures, they were sometimes barely secured in place.

Beyond this city of brick, stone and iron was a city of rickety wooden structures stretching for mile upon mile, a tinder-dry fuse waiting to be lit. De Koven Street, in a working-class neighborhood on the Southwest Side, was a part of this fuse. Its cottages were all of wood. Nearby was more wood: planing mills, chair factories, lumberyards, and the rolling stock of the vast railroad network that served the Queen City of the Prairie.

Curiously, much of legend of how the Great Chicago Fire began is true. It did in fact break out in a small barn behind Patrick O'Leary's cottage at 137 De Koven Street. The cottage was in what was then officially called "The West Division"—the portion of Chicago which lay to the west of the south branch of the Chicago River. Whether or not a cow did indeed kick over a lantern in the barn is impossible to say, but there were a cow and a lantern in the shed where the blaze started. Conditions were just about perfect for a fire. The summer and fall had been inordinately dry. From July 3 till October 9 there had been but 2½ inches of rain, compared to an average of more than 8 inches in previous years. This lack of rainfall had already led to devastating forest fires in the neighboring states of Michigan and Wisconsin, as well as a number of serious fires in Chicago itself. On October 7, the day before the Great Fire, four blocks of the city had burned; fighting the flames had left the fire department so exhausted that it was slow in responding to the alarm from De Koven Street. When it did so it was too late. By 10:30 it was officially reported that the fire was out of control, but most of the citizens of Chicago calmly finished their day and went to bed thinking that the bright orange glow in the western sky was just another fire, a big one, true, but no more important than the hundreds of others that had plagued the city during the past few years. Though they didn't know it, Chicago's doom was sealed. There was a deadly force behind this particular fire. Out of the southwest a strong, dry wind was blowing off the prairie, driving the fire toward the heart of the city. It was this steady wind, powerful as a bellows, that men such as Mayor William B. Ogden remembered years afterwards. Some called it a devilish wind.

At 11:30, after having reduced the wooden warrens of the West Side to ashes, the fire leapt the Chicago River into the South Side, the center of the city.

OVER: *Plate 1. A bird's-eye view of Chicago from Lake Michigan as it was before the Great Fire of 1871 shows the mouth of the Chicago River in the center of the picture, with the city's North Side on the right and the South Side on the left.* (Harper's Weekly, *October 21, 1871*)

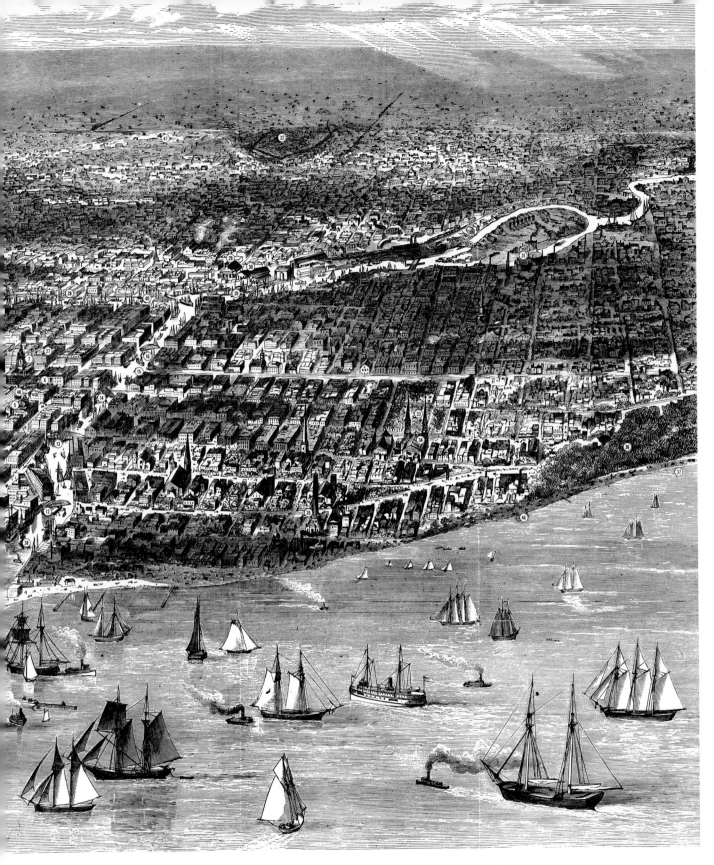

Among the first buildings to be devoured was the new stable of the Parmalee Omnibus and Stage Company at the southeast corner of Jackson and Franklin Streets. Soon the gasworks was ablaze as were the ornate banks and office blocks of the financial district along La Salle Street. By now Chicagoans were beginning to realize that this was no ordinary fire. In describing it, reporters fell back on military terms. "It was the onslaught of a cavalry corps on the retreating army's rear," the *Chicago Times* said. "The flames advanced like the charges of an army," the *Chicago Post* echoed. At times a dozen different locations were burning at once, as when Wells, Market, and Franklin Streets all blazed up. Sometimes 20 blocks and 500 buildings were aflame. When the reeling firemen and volunteers tried to make a stand, they were like footsoldiers armed with bows and arrows facing an enemy equipped with cannon. With terrible regularity the flames vaulted over their heads and set to work at their rear. When the barns near Harrison Street suddenly ignited behind the fire fighters, it was only by luck that the men escaped with their lives.

The highly vaunted "fire-proof" construction of buildings such as that of the *Tribune* at Dearborn and Madison Streets proved of no avail against the roaring holocaust. By morning the *Tribune* was a smoking shell. The fire devoured with equal ease the other edifices which had been Chicago's pride. One by one the great hotels fell—the Briggs House, the Sherman, the Palmer House, the Tremont, the brand-new Grand Pacific—and the theaters, including Hooley's, the Washington Street, and the sumptuous Crosby's Opera House. Nor were the rich emporiums along State Street spared. Field and Leiter's sparkling marble store with its two and a half million dollars' worth of merchandise was soon a blackened ruin. But the worst blow came at 2:30 Monday morning. The Courthouse, standing in the block bounded by La Salle, Clark, Randolph and Washington Streets, had been the focus of the city since its completion in 1853. The Courthouse bell had announced a thousand civic ceremonies, including, in 1865, Abraham Lincoln's lying-in-state beneath it. It had tolled in warning when the Great Fire began. At 2:30 the bell crashed to the ground from the Courthouse's blazing dome. Now the Courthouse itself was consumed and its passing marked the end of Old Chicago, the pre-Fire city.

Those caught up in the holocaust had a vivid sense of glimpsing Dante's *Inferno*. A reporter for the *Chicago Post* wrote:

> From the roof of a tall stable and warehouse to which the writer clambered, the sight was one of unparalleled sublimity and terror . . . He could feel the heat and smoke and hear the maddened Babel of sounds, and it required but little imagination to believe one's self looking over the adamantine bulwarks of hell into the bottomless pit.

For those who had been astonished by the swift ease with which the fire had eaten though the West and South Sides, there was yet another surprise in store. At 1:30 in the morning the State Street Bridge leading to the North Side began burning, and soon the sparks had gained a foothold in the district of the city north of the Chicago River. In short order stables, warehouses, grain elevators and breweries such as Lill's vast establishment were devoured. Then the hungry flames began working on the luxurious residential district centered around Cass, Huron, Ontario, Rush and Dearborn Streets where stood the mansions of some of Chicago's oldest and most prestigious families—the McCormicks, Trees, Kinzies, Arnolds, Rumseys and Ogdens. Long before daylight there was nothing but burnt-out shells where hours before silver had gleamed, oriental carpets had muffled the footfall and carved rosewood furniture had graced high parlors. By 3:00 the pumps of the Waterworks on Pine Street had been stilled. By the evening of Monday, the ninth, the only intact structure for miles was the yellow-stone Gothic Water Tower.

It was not only the inexorable flames that the frightened, weary citizens had to face. Early in the course of the fire drunkeness and looting had broken out. Saloon keepers, hoping that it would prevent their premises from being sacked, had rolled barrels of whiskey into the streets and soon people of all classes, including many women, were staggering through the city driven by the thought that if this were indeed the end of the world they might as well have one last fling. The looting was on a scale with the fire. William S. Walker, a journalist, wrote:

> Before daybreak, the thieving horror had culminated in scenes of daring robbery, unparalleled in the annals of any similar disaster . . . as the night wore on, and the terrors aggregated into an intensity of misery, the thieves, amateur and professional, dropped all pretence of concealment and plied their knavish calling undaunted by any fears of immediate retribution. They would storm into stores, smash away at safes . . . Burglars would raid into private dwellings that lay in the track of the coming destruction, and snatch from the cupboard, bureau, trunk, and mantel, anything which their practical senses told them would be of value.

Yet the looters, like most of the other citizens of Chicago, miscalculated the extent and fierceness of the flames and much of their plunder was eventually dropped in the streets and burned as they themselves fled for their lives. This experience of chaotic lawlessness made a deep impression on respectable Chicagoans. It comes up time and again in the memoirs they wrote about the Great Fire. It is no wonder, then, that when General Philip Sheridan led his troops into the city on October eleventh and assumed full police authority he became an instant hero. "Thanks for your promptness," was the message sent to him by the relieved governor of Illinois, John Palmer.

The morning of the tenth saw the flames at last drowned by a steady rain. Shivering along the Lake Michigan shore, lying exhausted on the prairie to the west, huddled in the just-emptied cemetery which would become Lincoln Park, the people of Chicago surveyed their ruined city. The destruction that they saw was staggering. Three hundred were dead, 100,000 without shelter, a swath four miles long and two-thirds of a mile wide, 1,687 acres, had been burnt across the city. Almost $200 million in property had vanished. Records, deeds, libraries, archives and art galleries were all lost. Little survived in the vaults of the city's banks. In the destruction of the Federal Building alone, which had stood at the northwest corner of Dearborn and Monroe Streets and housed, among other things, the Post Office and Custom House, more than $1,000,000 in currency had been incinerated. It is no wonder that the *New York Tribune* said of the charred wasteland that had but shortly before been a great metropolis: "It is the greatest and most brilliant apparition of the nineteenth century." It is no wonder that John Greenleaf Whittier's poem on the fire achieved instant popularity. Its first two stanzas are:

> Men said at vespers: "All is well!"
> In one wild night the city fell;
> Fell shrines of prayer and marts of grain
> Before the fiery hurricane.

> On threescore spires had sunset shone,
> Where ghastly sunrise looked on none.
> Men clasped each other's hands, and said:
> "The City of the West is dead!"

Of course Chicago was not dead; it was merely stunned. Within days it began rebuilding on an extravagant scale. The historian Alfred T. Andreas in his *History of Chicago* captures the immensity of the undertaking:

> It is common to see ten or a dozen or fifty houses rising at once; but when one looks upon, not a dozen or fifty, but upon ten thousand houses rising and ten times that number of busy workmen coming and going, and listens to the noise of countless saws and hammers and chisels and axes and planes, he is bewildered.

The vigor with which Chicago rebuilt bewildered the entire nation, and in the short span of three years it once more dominated the West. Out of the incredible nerve of this fresh, new metropolis sprang the great gifts Chicago would make to America and to the world: steel-framed skyscrapers and prairie houses; realistic literature and *Poetry* magazine; jazz and the White City. The names associated with these things would become part of the American legend: Louis Sullivan and Frank Lloyd Wright; Theodore Dreiser and Edgar Lee Masters; Louis Armstrong and Daniel Burnham.

DAVID LOWE

Blackened and bleeding, helpless, panting, prone
On the charred fragments of her shattered throne
Lies she who stood but yesterday alone.

Queen of the West! by some enchanter taught
To lift the glory of Aladdin's court,
Then lose the spell that all that wonder wrought.

Like her own prairies by some chance seed sown,
Like her own prairies in one brief day grown,
Like her own prairies in one fierce night mown.

She lifts her voice, and in her pleading call
We hear the cry of Macedon to Paul—
The cry for help that makes her kin to all.

But haply with wan fingers may she feel
The silver cup hid in the proffered meal—
The gifts her kinship and our loves reveal.

BRET HARTE

Joseph Edgar Chamberlin

[At the time of the fire, Chamberlin was a reporter of twenty on the old *Chicago Evening Post,* afterward consolidated with the *Evening Mail.* His account was first published in *Chicago and the Great Conflagration,* issued soon after the fire by Elias Colbert and Everett Chamberlin.]

I was at the scene in a few minutes. The fire had already advanced a distance of about a single square through the frame buildings that covered the ground thickly north of De Koven Street and east of Jefferson Street—if those miserable alleys shall be dignified by being denominated streets [Plate 2]. That neighborhood had always been a terra incognita to respectable Chicagoans, and during a residence of three years in the city I had never visited it. The land was thickly studded with one-story frame dwellings, cow stables, pigsties, corncribs, sheds innumerable; every wretched building within four feet of its neighbor, and everything of wood—not a brick or a stone in the whole area.

The fire was under full headway in this combustible mass before the engines arrived, and what could be done? Streams were thrown into the flame, and evaporated almost as soon as they struck it [Plate 3]. A single fire engine in the blazing forests of Wisconsin would have been as effective as were these machines in a forest of shanties thrice as combustible as the pine woods of the North. But still the firemen kept

Plate 2. The Patrick O'Leary house on De Koven Street on the Southwest Side in 1871. The Great Fire is supposed to have started in a barn behind the house. (Courtesy of the Chicago Historical Society)

at work fighting the flames—stupidly and listlessly, for they had worked hard all of Saturday night and most of Sunday, and had been enervated by the whisky which is always copiously poured on such occasions. I stepped in among some sheds south of Ewing Street; a fence by my side began to blaze; I beat a hasty retreat, and in five minutes the place where I had stood was all ablaze. Nothing could stop that conflagration there. It must sweep on until it reached a broad street, and then, everybody said, it would burn itself out.

Ewing Street was quite a thoroughfare for that region. It is a mere alley, it is true, but is somewhat broader than the surrounding lanes. It has elevated board sidewalks, and is passable for teams in dry weather. On that night it was crowded with people pouring out of the thickly-settled locality between Jefferson Street and the river, and here the first panic began. The wretched female inhabitants were rushing out almost naked, imploring spectators to help them on with their burdens of bed quilts, cane-bottomed chairs, iron kettles, etc. Drays were thundering along in the single procession which the narrowness of the street allowed, and all was confusion.

When the fire had passed Ewing Street, I hurried on to Harrison, aware of the fact that the only hope

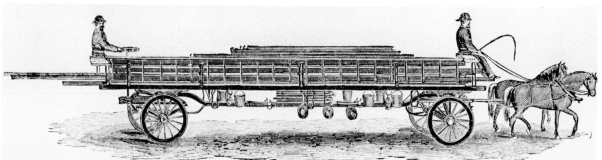

Plate 3. *Equipment of the type used by the Chicago Fire Department at the time of the Great Fire.* TOP: *A "steamer," a steam fire engine consisting of a boiler, engine and pump.* MIDDLE: *A hook and ladder.* BOTTOM: *A typical hose cart. (From* Report of Board of Police on Fire Department, *1872, courtesy of the Chicago Historical Society)*

Plate 4. *The ruins of the armory and gasworks, as seen from the corner of Franklin and Adams Streets. (Courtesy of the Chicago Historical Society)*

for the staying of the conflagration was in the width of that street, and hoping that some more effective measures than squirting of water would be taken at that point. The same scene of hurry and confusion was repeated at Harrison on a larger scale than at Ewing; and that same scene kept on increasing in terror all night long as the fire moved northward. The crowd anxiously watched the flames as they approached the street, and the universal remark was: "If it passes this, nothing can stop it but last night's burned district." At length the fire reached the street, and broke out almost simultaneously for a distance of two squares. The two fire engines which stood in Harrison Street fled in terror. Brands of fire driven on by the gale struck the houses on the north side of the street. Though mostly of brick, they ignited like tinder, and the fire swept northward again.

Again I passed into Jefferson Street, keeping on the flank of the fire. In a vacant square filled with refugees from the fire and their rescued effects I stopped a few minutes to watch the fiery ocean before me. The open lot was covered with people, and a strange sight was presented. The fire had reached a better section, and many people of the better class were among those who had gathered a few of their household goods on that open space. Half a dozen rescued pianos were watched by delicate ladies, while the crowd still surged in every direction. Two boys, themselves intoxicated, reeled about, each bearing a small cask of whisky out of which he insisted upon treating everybody he met. Soon more casks of whisky appeared, and scores of excited men drank deeply of their contents. The result was, of course, that an equal number of drunken men were soon impeding the flight of the fugitives.

When I reached Van Buren Street, the southern limit of the Saturday night fire, I paused to see the end of the conflagration. A single engine stood on Van Buren Street, doing what seemed to me good service in preventing the fire from eating its way westward, against the wind, which it was apparently determined to do. Suddenly the horses were attached to the engine, and as soon as the hose was reeled it disappeared, whirling northward on Jefferson Street. What did it mean? I caught the words, "across the river," uttered doubtingly by a bystander. The words passed from mouth to mouth, and there was universal incredulity, although the suggestion was communicated through the crowd with startling rapidity.

There was a general movement northward and out of the smoke, with a view to discover whether it was really possible that the fire had been blown across the river, and had started afresh on the south side. I went with the rest, crossed the burnt ground of the night before, stood on the embankment that had been Canal Street, and perceived, through the clouds of smoke, a bright light across the river. I rushed to the Adams Street viaduct and across the bridge. The Armory, the Gasworks [Plate 4], "Conley's Patch," and Wells Street as far north as Monroe were all on fire. The wind had increased to a tempest, and hurled great blazing brands over our heads.

At this point my duty called me to my home in the West Division; but within an hour I was back again to witness the doom of the blazing city, of which I then had a full presentiment. The streets on the West Side were as light as broad noon. I looked at my watch and saw that it was just two o'clock. As I ran down Monroe Street, with the burning town before me, I contemplated the ruin that was working, and the tears arose to my eyes. I could have wept at the saddest of sights, but I choked down the tears, and they did not rise again that night.

When I crossed the river, I made a desperate attempt to reach my office on Madison Street beyond Clark. I pressed through the crowd on Randolph Street as far as La Salle, and stood in front of the burning Courthouse [Plates 5–7]. The cupola was in full blaze, and presented a scene of the sublimest as well as most melancholy beauty. Presently the great tower was undermined by the fire below, and fell to the bottom with a dull sound and a heavy shock that shook the earth. Somebody called out, "Explosion!" and a panic ensued in which everything and everybody was carried westward. Then I went to Lake

Plate 5. The Courthouse, standing in the block bounded by La Salle, Clark, Randolph and Washington Streets, from the northwest as it appeared about 1868. (Photograph by John Carbutt, courtesy of the Chicago Historical Society)

Street, and found a torrent of sparks sweeping down that avenue. But I pulled my hat about my eyes, buttoned up my coat collar, and rushed eastward, determined to reach my office. I turned down Dearborn, and leaped through a maelstrom of scorching sparks. The fiery storm at length drove me into an open store, from which the occupants had fled. I seized a large blanket which they had left on the floor, wrapped it around my head and body, and sallied forth again. I went as far as Washington Street, but any attempt at further progress would have been madness. I beat a hasty retreat to Lake Street, and came down La Salle again to the immediate neighborhood of the fire.

And now the scene of confusion had reached its height. Wagons were rushing through the streets laden with stocks of goods, books, valuable papers, boxes of money, and everything conceivable; scores of men were dragging trunks frantically along the sidewalks, knocking down women and children; fabulous sums of money were offered truckmen for conveyances. The scene was indescribable.

But, as large as was the number of people who were flying from the fire, the number of passive spectators was still larger. Their eyes were all diverted from the skurrying mass of people around them to the spectacle of appalling grandeur before them. They stood transfixed, with a mingled feeling of horror and admiration, and while they often exclaimed at the beauty of the scene, they all devoutly prayed that they might never see such another.

The noise of the conflagration was terrific. To the roar which the simple process of combustion always makes, magnified here to so grand an extent, was added the crash of falling buildings and the constant explosions of stores of oil and other like material. The noise of the crowd was nothing compared with this chaos of sound. All these things—the great, dazzling, mounting light, the crash and roar of the conflagration, and the desperate flight of the crowd—combined to make a scene of which no intelligent idea can be conveyed in words.

When it became too hot in Randolph Street, I retired to the eastern approach of the bridge on that street. A knot of men had gathered there, from whom all signs of excitement had disappeared. It was then almost four o'clock, and whatever excitement we had felt during the night had passed away. Wearied with two nights of exertion, I sat upon the railing and looked down on the most appalling spectacle of the whole night. The Briggs House, the Metropolitan House, Peter Schuttler's wagon manufactory, Heath & Milligan's oil establishment stored five stories high with exceedingly inflammable material, the Nevada Hotel, and all the surrounding buildings, were in a simultaneous blaze [Plate 8]. The flames, propelled by variable gusts of wind, seemed to pour down Randolph Street in a liquid torrent. Then the appearance

ABOVE: *Plate 6.* *The Courthouse in flames.* (Frank Leslie's Illustrated Newspaper, *October 28, 1871*) BELOW: *Plate 7. Looking east on Randolph Street after the fire with the gutted Courthouse on the right. (Courtesy of the Chicago Historical Society)*

Plate 8. The scene on Wells Street in front of the Briggs House, one of the city's luxurious hotels that burned. (Frank Leslie's Illustrated Newspaper, *October 28, 1871*)

Plate 9. *The Rush Street Bridge, a key north-south link across the Chicago river, is seen as it appeared during the Civil War in this lithograph by Edwin Whitefield. The English-born Whitefield, who did seven views of the city, lived in Chicago from 1860 to 1864. (From Edwin Whitefield's* Views of Chicago, *courtesy of the Chicago Historical Society)*

was changed, and the fire was a mountain over our heads. The barrels of oil in Heath's store exploded with a sound like rattling musketry. The great north wall of the Nevada Hotel plunged inward with hardly a sound, so great was the din of the surrounding conflagration. The Garden City House burned like a box of matches; the rapidity of its disappearance was remarked by everybody. Toward the east and northeast we looked upon a surging ocean of flame.

Meanwhile a strange scene was being enacted in the street before us. A torrent of humanity was pouring over the bridge [Plates 9 and 10]. The Madison Street bridge had long before become impassable, and Randolph was the only outlet for the entire region south of it. Drays, express wagons, trucks, and conveyances of every conceivable species and size crowded across in indiscriminate haste. Collisions happened almost every moment, and when one overloaded wagon broke down, there were enough men on hand to drag it and its contents over the bridge by main force.

The same long line of men dragging trucks was there, many of them tugging over the ground with loads which a horse would strain at. Women were there, looking exactly like those I had seen all night, staggering under weights upon their backs. Whole establishments of ill-fame were there, their half-dozen inmates loaded into the bottom of express wagons, driven, of course, by their "men." Now and then a stray schooner, which, for want of a tug, had been unable to escape earlier from the South Branch, came up, and the bridge must be opened. Then arose a howl of indignation along the line, which, being near,

was audible above the tumult. A brig lay above us in the stream, and the captain was often warned by the crowd that he must make his exit at once, if he wished to save his craft—a suggestion the force of which he doubtless appreciated, as he stood upon the quarter-deck calling frantically to every tug that passed.

I saw an undertaker rushing over the bridge with his mournful stock. He had taken a dray, but was unable to load all of his goods into the vehicle, so he employed half a dozen boys, gave each of them a coffin, took a large one himself, and headed the weird procession. The sight of those coffins, upright, and bobbing along just above the heads of the crowd, without any apparent help from anybody else, was somewhat startling, and the unavoidable suggestion was that they were escaping across the river to be ready for use when the debris of the conflagration should be cleared away. But just as men in the midst of a devastating plague carouse over each new corpse, and drink to the next who dies, so we laughed quite merrily at the ominous spectacle.

At last it became too warm to be comfortable on the east side of the river. The fire was burning along Market Street, and many were the conjectures whether Lind's Block would go. The buildings opposite burned with a furnace heat, but Lind's Block stands now, a monument to its own isolation.

And then the question was everywhere asked, "Will Chicago ever recover from this blow?" Many suggestions were offered on this subject. The general

OVER: *Plate 10. Throngs flee northward over the Randolph Street Bridge.* (Harper's Weekly, *October 28, 1871*)

opinion was that the city could never again obtain a foothold. Said one old gentleman, ''Our capital is wiped out of existence. You never can get what money is stored up out of those vaults. There isn't one that can stand this furnace heat. Whatever the fire consumes tonight is utterly consumed. All loss is total; for there will not be an insurance company left tomorrow. The trade of the city *must* go to St. Louis, to Cincinnati; and to New York, and we never can get hold of it again. We couldn't transact any business even if we had customers, for we haven't got anywhere to transact it. Yes, sir, this town is gone up, and we may as well get out of it at once.'' Thus all seemed to talk, and there was none of that earnest, hopeful language of which I have heard so much since, and have been rejoiced to hear. But what else could I expect? These men stood facing the burning city. They saw those great hotels and warehouses toppling, one after another, to the ground. Their spirits were elastic, as subsequent events have proved, but on that terrible night they were drawn to their utmost tension, and the cord came near breaking.

Tired with my two nights' work, and of the sad sight before me, I joined the crowd, crossed the river, went up Canal Street and lay down on a pile of lumber in Avery's yard. My position was at the confluence of the North and South branches, directly opposite the middle of the main river, and exactly on the dock. All solicitude for the remaining portion of the city, and all appreciation of the magnitude of the tragedy that was being acted across the river, had left me. I did not care whether the city stood or burned. I was dead so far as my sensibilities were concerned. Half a dozen fellows—strangers—were with me on the lumber pile, and were as listless as myself. The chief matter which seemed to interest them was the probable weight of one of their party—a fat fellow whom they called Fred. I became quite interested in

the subject, and joined in the guessing. Fred kept us bursting in ignorance awhile, and then, in a burst of confidence, told us he weighed 206, and begged us not to mention it.

Meanwhile, Wells Street bridge took fire, and, as affording something novel, attracted our attention for a few minutes. The south end of the bridge caught alight, and then the north end. But the north end burned less rapidly than the south, and soon outbalanced the latter, when, of course, the whole structure tipped to the northward, and stood poised, one end in the water, at an angle of about sixty degrees. Then the fire communicated with the whole framework, till the bridge looked like a skeleton with ribs of fire. But presently the support underneath burned away, then the skeleton turned a complete somersault and plunged into the river, as if it warmed into life it had sought refuge from the flames which were consuming it.

When I had regained a footing in the favored West Division it was seven o'clock. Then a curious-looking crimson ball came up out of the lake, which they said was the sun; but oh, how sickly and insignificant it looked! I had watched that greatest of the world's conflagrations from its beginning to almost its end, and although the fire was still blazing all over the city with undiminished luster, I could not look at it. I was almost unable to walk with exhaustion and the effects of a long season of excitement, and sought my home for an hour's sleep. As I passed up West Madison Street, I met scores of working girls on their way ''down town'' as usual, bearing their lunch baskets, as if nothing had happened. They saw the fire and smoke before them, but could not believe that the city, with their means of livelihood, had been swept away during that night.

On Sunday night, October 8, I was at the Sherman House [Plate 11]. I went there, at the request of my sister, to see if some of her friends who were expected from Milwaukee had arrived, but was prevented by unexpected business. There was a large crowd of strangers and business men of the city at the hotel. The corridor and parlors were full of idlers, much as usual. While looking over the register someone said, ''There go the fire bells again''; and the remark was made jocosely, ''They'll burn the city down if they keep on.'' I paid little attention to the conversation, which did not interest me, and having ascertained that the names that I wanted were not on the register I sauntered in the corridor awhile, and meeting Mr. Nixon, the upholsterer on Lake Street, I sat down a moment.

Mr. Nixon made the mistake of pointing out to me a person whom I knew very well by sight, and who lived in Chicago, insisting that it was George Francis Train; and while we were disputing about it, my nephew, a young man of eighteen, came up, and I appealed to him to identify the person. He then told us that a big fire was burning on the West Side. I asked him if he would mind walking to Ewing Street, where my sister was stopping, and letting her know that her friends were not in town; but he replied that I had better go myself, because the fire was in that vicinity, and he had a friend waiting for him upstairs.

When I came down the wind was blowing fiercely through Clark Street to the river, and I had some difficulty in getting across the Courthouse square. It could not have been ten o'clock, for they were singing in the Methodist church as I passed Follansbee's bank. I noticed the glare of the fire on the West Side as I came along, but thought nothing of it. There were very few people out, and I did not meet with a policeman until I reached Monroe Street. He was walking rapidly towards me, and I asked him if he knew anything about the fire; he looked at me but made no reply, and kept hurrying on. There was a small party of men on the corner of Adams Street. I asked them

the same question, and one of them said, ''It must be a damn big fire this time; you can't put out a high wind with water.'' The rest of them said nothing, but I thought they looked a little scared. While I stood there a policeman came up Adams Street on horseback and turned into Clark Street. Some of them hallooed to him, but he paid no attention. I kept on, but before I had reached the next street the cinders began to fall thick and fast all around me, and it was growing lighter all the time.

A great many people were looking out of their windows, and the streets seemed to get full of people suddenly. They were not excited. They stood about in groups listening to the wind, that was making a noise very much like the lake on a stormy night.

I went into a Dutch beer saloon to get a cigar, seeing the door half open. The gas was burning, but the persons who kept the place were all in the street. I helped myself to a cigar from an open box that stood on the counter and left a stamp for it; lighting it at the gas burner I went out without being questioned. When I was holding it up to the gas jet I noticed for the first time that I was considerably excited myself; my hand shook and I could hear my heart beat. I don't think I was two minutes in the place, but when I came out the cinders were falling like snowflakes in every direction and lit the street, and there was a great hubbub of men and vehicles.

I started to run toward Van Buren Street, but the walks were so crowded with people and the cinders were blown so thickly and fast that I found it was impossible. Besides, the wind blew my hat off twice. I took to the middle of the street, and found that the crowd coming from the opposite direction was increasing. But it was difficult to see anything on account of the cinders. Somewhere between Van Buren and Polk streets I found the crowd jammed into the thoroughfare solidly. There was a four-story brick house on the east side that overlooked the others all around it. A man on top seemed to be gesticulating and shouting to the crowd, but whatever he said was lost in the wind. It was some time before I made out

Alexander Frear

[Frear was a member of the Assembly of the State of New York, Commissioner of Public Charities, and a Commissioner of Emigration in the City of New York. His account appeared in the *New York World*, October 15, 1871.]

around with the purpose of running to the first

No sooner did I understand that it was impossible and dangerous to proceed farther, and had turned the throng.

that he was shouting to someone in a window below, and the man below repeated it to the crowd. All I could distinctly hear was, ''burning on both sides of the river,'' and just then there was a great pressure in the crowd of the people and a man on horseback forced his way through. He seemed to be a gentleman, and I thought an insurance officer. He had in his hand one of the little red flags that switchmen use, which he waved on either side. What he said I could not hear, but it had the effect of producing a panic in

bridge, than I saw the light of the fire extending far back in the direction I had come, the flames lighting the houses on the east side of Clark Street as far as I could see. I ran as fast as I could to the Adams Street bridge. Vehicles and people were streaming in from all the streets to the west. I paid little attention to anything, my anxiety to reach my sister's house being very great. With difficulty I got to the bridge, which was beset by teams desiring to cross, and tugs scream-ing in the stream to get through. There was much confusion, and suddenly a rush of people was made toward me as the bridge began to swing, and I ran to get over. A woman, carrying a bureau drawer, and

blinded by the sparks, in her desperation struck me in the breast with her burden, breaking the crystal of my watch and stunning me for a moment. It was 11:30 o'clock; while I held my watch in my hand a live coal fell on it as large as a silver half-dollar. All of Adams Street reaching to Des Plaines on the West Side was choked with people, but they were free from the terrible rain of cinders, the wind carrying them in a northeasterly direction across the river [Plate 12]. Des Plaines Street was comparatively clear, and on turning into it I lost my hat. Without attempting to recover it I ran as fast as I could in the direction of Ewing Street.

My sister's house was out of the line of the fire, but there was no telling at what moment the wind would veer. My brother, who is a lumber merchant, was absent in Sheboygan. The house was occupied by his family, consisting of Mrs. Frear and the three children (two girls and a boy, all of them under fifteen years of age, the youngest, Johnny, a cripple with rheumatism), and a lodger, who was employed as a clerk in Mr. Frear's office. The family was in great consternation. I told Mrs. Frear that I thought there was no present danger, as the fire was not burning this side of Jefferson Street, but was being blown swiftly to the east. We were within a block, however, of Jefferson Street, and the heat was intense, and the excitement of the neighborhood very great. I found that she had her clothing and valuables all packed in trunks, which were pulled into the hallway; and she told me that Mr. Wood, the clerk, had gone to get one of Mr. Farwell's trucks to take her things to the warehouse on Wabash Avenue, she saying she would remain and look after the house until the danger was over.

Fortunately there was not much trouble in getting a coach, and I started as soon after as possible with the three children. The Kimballs were all abed, and I was some time ringing at the door, holding Johnny wrapped in a rug, before I roused them.

The driver of the horses put his horses to their utmost speed in returning. When we reached the vicinity of Madison Street bridge he threw the door open and said we couldn't get across. The noise of the men and vehicles was so great that he had to shout at the top of his voice. We then drove up to Randolph Street, and here we were stopped again, the bridge being open. It seemed that the string of vessels passing through was endless. We were an hour and a half in getting back, I think. The whole of Ewing Street was barricaded with vehicles and household effects.

Mrs. Frear was much cooler now that her children were safe. Most of her valuables had been got off, and as it was no longer possible to get a dray up to the house, the heavy furniture had to remain. While we were talking Mr. Wood burst into the room, and said that the fire had reached Wabash Avenue and was sweeping all before it. His appearance as well as his language was terrifying. Nearly blinded by the flying embers he had dashed water on his head and face, and his matted hair and begrimed skin added to his frightened looks made him seem like another person.

I begged Mrs. Frear not to alarm herself, and ran up to the roof. The house was a two-story-and-a-half frame building, but it joined another which was an addition to a planing mill. I clambered to the roof of the latter, and was nearly swept off by the wind. As near as I could make out Wood was right. . . . Wherever I could see at all the wind blew the burning houses into a mass of live coals that was dazzling. When I returned I found Mrs. Frear had her waterproof cloak on, and had put her jewelry and money into a satchel and was ready to start. I begged of her to remain, saying that I would see to the safety of the children, but she only answered, "My poor Johnny, my poor sick Johnny."

Mr. Wood and myself then endeavored to get another conveyance. The front steps and the sidewalks were thronged with terror-stricken women, and the street was encumbered with luggage. The three of us fought our way through . . . till we reached Mr. McGowan's in Halsted Street, and here we were fortunate enough to get a cab. Wood then went back to the house, and we started for Wabash Avenue, Mr. McGowan himself driving. I afterwards found out that he had to take us all the way to Clark Street on the North Side to get over the river, but at the time I did not notice our direction until we had crossed the river, being occupied in trying to pacify Mrs. Frear. We got as far as Washington Street in the Avenue when McGowan was stopped and got into an altercation with an officer. . . . I sprang out and was told that it was useless to go any farther, for the whole of the Avenue was on fire. The roadway was full of people, and the din of voices and the melee of horses rendered unmanageable by the falling embers was terrible.

In the confusion it was difficult to get any information; but I was told that the block in which the Kimballs lived [the refuge of Mrs. Frear's children] was burning, and that the people were all out. To add to my distress, Mrs. Frear jumped out of the vehicle and started to run in the direction of the fire. Nothing, I am satisfied, saved her from being crushed to death in a mad attempt to find her children but the providential appearance of an acquaintance, who told her that the children were all safe at the St. James Hotel.

When we reached the hotel I found it impossible to get her through the crowd without trouble, and so I took her into Soldan & Ward's hairdressing-room in the basement, and went upstairs to look for the children alone. There was a great deal of excitement in the house, but there seemed to be no apprehension of danger from the fire at that distance. The guests

and servants of the house were nearly all at the windows or down in the doorways. I found that Mrs. Frear's acquaintance had either intentionally or unintentionally deceived her. The children were not in the house. When I informed her of it she fainted. When she was being taken upstairs to the parlor I found she had lost her satchel. Whether it was left in the cab when she jumped out, or was stolen in the house, I cannot say. It contained two gold watches, several pins and drops of value, a cameo presented to her by Mrs. Stephen A. Douglas, a medal of honor belonging to her husband (who was an officer in the First Wisconsin Volunteers during the war), and

about $200 in bills and currency stamps, besides several trinkets of trifling value.

Leaving her in the care of some ladies, I then started for John V. Farwell's stores, on Wabash Avenue, thinking it possible the children were sent there, where their mother's property was. When I came into Wabash Avenue the full extent of the fire and its danger to the city became for the first time apparent to my mind. I saw the flames distinctly, and, remembering that they were two miles distant when I first saw them, I began to realize the awful nature of the calamity. I spoke to several persons on the street. They seemed to think the flames would be stayed when they reached the durable and massive structures, and that it was only the wooden buildings that caused such a furious burning.

The Farwell stores were all closed. The watchman said there had been no goods, much less children, brought there. I then ran as fast as I could through Randolph Street to Sherman House, thinking we might have mistaken the hotel. They had the hose laid on, and a party of men were on the roof putting out the cinders. I was told that the place had already been ignited twice. The corridor was a scene of intense excitement. The guests of the house were running about wildly, some of them dragging their trunks to the stairway. Everything was in confusion, and my heart sank within me as I saw the panic spreading among those who were the best protected. I looked out of one of the south windows of the house, and shall never forget the terribly magnificent sight I saw. The Courthouse Park was filled with people, who appeared to be huddled together in a solid mass, helpless and astounded [Plate 13]. The whole air was filled with the falling cinders, and it looked like a snowstorm lit by colored fire. The weird effect of the glare and the scintillating light upon this vast, silent concourse was almost frightful.

While in the corridor of the Sherman House I encountered my nephew, and he asked me if I wanted to see the fire, saying he had one of George Garrison's horses and only wanted a rubber blanket to throw over him to protect him from the sparks. I told him about Mrs. Frear, but he thought there was no reason to worry. He got a blanket somewhere, and we started off in a light wagon for Wabash Avenue, stopping at Wright's, under the Opera House, to get a drink of coffee, which I needed very much [Plate 14]. There were several of the firemen of the Little Giant[1] in there. One of the men was bathing his head with whisky from a flask. They declared that the entire department had given up, overworked, and that they could do nothing more.

While we stood there an Irish girl was brought in with her dress nearly all burnt from her person. It had caught on the Courthouse steps from a cinder. When we went out a man in his shirt-sleeves was unhitching the horse; and when we came up he sprang into the wagon, and would have driven off in spite of us if I had not caught the horse by the head. He then sprang out and struck my nephew in the face, and ran toward State Street.

We drove as rapidly as we could into Wabash Avenue, the wind sweeping the embers after us in furious waves. We passed a broken-down steamer[2] in the middle of the roadway. The avenue was a scene of desolation. The storm of falling fire seemed to increase every second, and it was as much as we could do to protect ourselves from the burning rain and guide the horse through the flying people and hurrying vehicles.

Looking back through Washington Street, toward

the Opera House, I saw the smoke and flames pouring out of State Street, from the very point we had just left, and the intervening space was filled with the whirling embers that beat against the houses and covered the roofs and windowsills. It seemed like a tornado of fire. To add to the terrors, the animals, burnt and infuriated by the cinders, darted through the streets regardless of all human obstacles. Wabash Avenue was burning as far down as Adams Street. The flames from the houses on the west side reached in a diagonal arch quite across the street, and occasionally the wind would lift the great body of flame, detach it entirely from the burning buildings, and hurl it with terrific force far ahead.

All the mansions were being emptied with the greatest disorder and the greatest excitement. Nobody endeavored to stay the flames now. A mob of men and women, all screaming and shouting, ran about wildly, crossing each other's paths, and intercepting each other as if deranged. We tried to force our way along the avenue, which was already littered with costly furniture, some of it burning in the streets under the falling sparks, but it was next to impossible. Twice we were accosted by gentlemen with pocketbooks in their hands, and asked to carry away to a place of safety some valuable property. Much as we may have desired to assist them, it was out of our power. Women came and threw packages into the vehicle, and one man with a boy hanging to him caught the horse and tried to throw us out. I finally got out and endeavored to lead the animal out of the terrible scenes.

When we had gone about a block I saw that the Courthouse was on fire, and almost at the same moment someone said the St. James had caught on the roof. I was struck on the arm by a bird cage flung from an upper window, and the moment I released the horse he shied and ran into a burning dray-load of furniture, smashing the wheel of the wagon and throwing my companion out on his shoulder. Fortunately he was only bruised. But the horse, already terrified, started immediately, and I saw him disappear with a leap like that of a panther.

We then hurried on toward the St. James Hotel, passing through some of the strangest and saddest scenes it has ever been my misfortune to witness. I saw a woman kneeling in the street with a crucifix held up before her and the skirt of her dress burning while she prayed. We had barely passed before a runaway truck dashed her to the ground. Loads of goods passed us repeatedly that were burning on the trucks, and my nephew says that he distinctly saw one man go up to a pile of costly furniture lying in front of an elegant residence and deliberately hold a piece of burning packing board under it until the pile was lit.

When we reached the wholesale stores north of Madison Street the confusion was even worse. These

[1] The first engine to turn a stream on the fire at Mrs. O'Leary's barn, under John Campion's direction.

[2] Fire engine.

Plate 14. *The burning of Crosby's Opera House on the north side of Washington Street between Dearborn and State Streets.* (Harper's Weekly, *October 28, 1871*)

stores were packed full of the most costly merchandise, and to save it at the rate the fire was advancing was plainly impossible. There were no police, and no effort was made to keep off the rabble. A few of the porters and draymen employed by these stores were working manfully; but there were costermongers' wagons, dirt carts, and even coaches backed up and receiving goods, and a villainous crowd of men and boys chaffing each other and tearing open parcels to discover the nature of their contents.

I reached the St. James between two and three o'clock on Monday morning. It was reported to be on fire, but I did not see the flames then. Mrs. Frear had been moved in an insensible state to the house of a friend on the North Side. I could learn no other particulars.

The house was in a dreadful state of disorder. Women and children were screaming, in every direction, and baggage being thrown about in the most reckless manner. I now concluded that Mrs. Frear's children had been lost. It was reported that hundreds of people had perished in the flames.

There was a crowd of men and women at the hotel from one of the large boardinghouses in the neighborhood of State and Adams streets, and they said they barely escaped with their lives, leaving everything behind. At this time it seemed to me that the fire would leave nothing. People coming in said the Sherman House was going, and that the Opera House had caught. Finally, word was brought that the bridges were burning, and all escape was cut off to the north and west. Then ensued a scene which was beyond description. Men shouted the news and added to the panic. Women, half-dressed, and many of them with screaming children, fled out of the building. There was a jam in the doorway, and they struck and clawed

Plate 15. *The fire at the Tremont House, another notable Chicago hotel, which stood at the corner of Lake and Dearborn Streets.* (Frank Leslie's Illustrated Newspaper, October 28, 1871)

each other as if in self-defense. I lost sight of my nephew at this time.

Getting out with the crowd, I started and ran round toward the Tremont House [Plate 15]. Reaching Dearborn Street, the gust of fire was so strong that I could hardly keep my feet. I ran on down toward the Tremont. Here the same scene was being enacted with tenfold violence. The elevator had got jammed, and the screams of the women on the upper floors were heartrending. I forced my way upstairs, seeing no fire, and looked into all the open rooms, calling aloud the names of Mrs. Frear's daughters. Women were swarming in the parlors; invalids, brought there for safety, were lying upon the floor. Others were running distracted about, calling upon their husbands. Men, pale and awestruck and silent, looked on

without any means of averting the mischief.

All this time the upper part of the house was on fire. The street was choked with people, yelling and moaning with excitement and fright. I looked down upon them from an upper window a moment, and saw far up Dearborn Street the huge flames pouring in from the side streets I had traversed but an hour ago, and it appeared to me that they were impelled with the force of a tremendous blowpipe. Everything that they touched melted. Presently the smoke began to roll down the stairways, and almost immediately after the men who had been at work on the roof came running down. They made no outcry, but hurried from the house as if for their lives. I went up to the fourth story, looking into every room and kicking open those that were locked. There were several other men searching in the same manner, but I did not notice them. While up here, I obtained a view of the conflagration. It was advancing steadily upon the hotel from two or three points. There was very little smoke; it burned too rapidly, or what there was must have been carried away on the wind. The whole was accompanied by a crackling noise as of an enormous bundle of dry twigs burning, and by explosions that followed each other in quick succession on all sides.

When I was going down I found one of the men dragging an insensible woman downstairs by her shoulders. She was an unusually large woman, and had on a striped satin dress and a great quantity of jewelry, which I supposed she had put upon her person for safety. I assisted him to carry her down, and when she reached the lower story, to my surprise she suddenly recovered her consciousness and ran away followed by the man.

From the street entrance I could see up Dearborn Street as far as the Portland Block, and it was full of people all the distance, swaying and surging under the rain of fire. Around on Lake Street the tumult was worse. Here for the first time I beheld scenes of violence that made my blood boil. In front of Shay's magnificent dry-goods store a man loaded a store-truck with silks in defiance of the employees of the place. When he had piled all he could upon the truck, someone with a revolver shouted to him not to drive away or he would fire at him, to which he replied, "Fire, and be damned!" and the man put the pistol in his pocket again. Just east of this store there was at least a ton of fancy goods thrown into the street, over which the people and vehicles passed with utter indifference, until they took fire.

I saw a ragamuffin on the Clark Street bridge, who had been killed by a marble slab thrown from a window, with white kid gloves on his hands, and whose pockets were stuffed with gold-plated sleeve buttons; and on that same bridge I saw an Irish woman leading a goat that was big with young by one arm, while under the other she carried a piece of silk.

Lake Street was rich with treasure, and hordes of thieves forced their way into the stores and flung out the merchandise to their fellows in the street, who received it without disguise, and fought over it openly.

I went through to Wabash Avenue, and here the thoroughfare was utterly choked with all manner of goods and people. Everybody who had been forced from the other end of the town by the advancing flames had brought some article with him, and, as further progress was delayed, if not completely stopped by the river—the bridges of which were also choked—most of them, in their panic, abandoned their burdens, so that the streets and sidewalks presented the most astonishing wreck. Valuable oil paintings, books, pet animals, musical instruments, toys, mirrors, and bedding, were trampled under foot. Added to this, the goods from the stores had been hauled out and had taken fire, and the crowd, breaking into a liquor establishment, were yelling with the fury of demons, as they brandished champagne and brandy bottles.

The brutality and horror of the scene made it sickening. A fellow standing on a piano declared that the fire was the friend of the poor man. He wanted everybody to help himself to the best liquor he could get, and continued to yell from the piano until someone as drunk as himself flung a bottle at him and knocked him off it.

In this chaos were hundreds of children, wailing and crying for their parents. One little girl, in particular, I saw, whose golden hair was loose down her back and caught afire. She ran screaming past me, and somebody threw a glass of liquor upon her, which flared up and covered her with a blue flame.

It was impossible to get through to the bridge, and I was forced to go back toward Randolph Street. There was a strange and new fascination in the scenes that I could not resist. It was now daylight, and the fire was raging closely all about me. The Courthouse, the Sherman House, the Tremont House, and the wholesale stores on Wabash Avenue, and the retail stores on Lake Street were burning. The cries of the multitude on the latter streets had now risen into a terrible roar, for the flames were breaking into the river streets.

I saw the stores of Messrs. Drake, Hamlin, and Farwell burn. They ignited suddenly all over in a manner entirely new to me, just as I have seen paper do that is held to the fire until it is scorched and breaks out in a flame. The crowds who were watching them greeted the combustion with terrible yells.

In one of the stores—I think it was Hamlin's—there were a number of men at the time on the several floors passing out goods, and when the flames blown over against it enveloped the building, they were lost to sight entirely; nor did I see any effort whatever made to save them, for the heat was so intense that everybody was driven as before a tornado from the vicinity of the buildings.

I now found myself carried by the throng back to near Lake Street, and determined, if possible, to get over the river [Plate 16]. I managed to accomplish this, after a severe struggle, and at the risk of my life. The rail of the bridge was broken away, and a number of small boats loaded with goods were passing down the stream. How many people were pushed over the bridge into the water I cannot tell. I myself saw one man stumble under a load of clothing and disappear; nor did the occupants of the boats pay the slightest attention to him nor to the crowd overhead, except to guard against anybody falling into their vessels.

Once over the river I felt safe. It seemed to me highly improbable that the fire would leap the stream, which at this point is the widest. Alas! those who were there told me that the flames of the burning storehouses on Water Street were blown into the windows on the opposite side, and that before the houses

Plate 16. *Destruction along the Chicago River at Lake and Market Streets. In the background a coal yard still smolders. The yards, which had been heaped with coal for the coming winter, continued to burn for several days after the fire. (Photograph by Joseph Battersby, courtesy of the Chicago Historical Society)*

that line the south side were half consumed those on the other were crackling and flaming with intensity. I went through North Water Street, meeting a frantic multitude teeming from each of the bridges and by a tiresome detour got round to the West Side. When I arrived at my sister's house I found my nephew there, who informed me that Mrs. Frear had been taken to a private house in Huron Street, and was perfectly safe and well cared for.

I was wet and scorched and bedraggled. My clothes were burnt full of holes on my arms and shoulders and back. I asked Wood to make some coffee, which he promised to do, and I fell down in the hallway and went to sleep. I could not have lain there half an hour when Wood awoke me, saying that the fire was sweeping everything before it in the direction of Lincoln Park, and that Mrs. Frear must be moved again. We both started out then, and walked and ran as fast as we could in the direction of the North Side.

It was about 8:30 o'clock. We could see across the river at the cross streets that where yesterday was a populous city was now a mass of smoking ruins. All the way round we encountered thousands of people; but the excitement had given way to a terrible grief and desolation. Des Plaines and the northern part of Jefferson Street were piled up twelve and fifteen feet high with goods. Luckily Wood knew where to find Mrs. Frear, and he arrived at the house just in time to get her into a baker's wagon, which Wood and I pulled for half a mile. She was in terrible condition, being hysterical, and when we were in Des Plaines Street again there came an omnibus, loaded with frightened children, through Lake Street. They were crying and screaming, and Mrs. Frear heard them and began to screech at the top of her voice. The man who was driving the omnibus stopped and yelled after us to know where we were taking that woman. It was impossible to get the wagon through the street on account of the goods, and so we were forced to go half a mile farther out of our way.

Once at home a number of neighbors came to her assistance, and about four o'clock in the afternoon word came from the Kimballs that the children were all safe out at Riverside. I spent the greater part of the day in searching for her property without avail. I have lost nothing myself by the fire but what I can recover, but on Monday afternoon I went to bed with a sick headache and a fever, which were the result of mental excitement rather than physical exposure.

Mrs. Alfred Hebard

[A cousin of Gurdon Saltonstall Hubbard, Mrs. Hebard had married Colonel Alfred Hebard in 1837, and they became pioneer settlers of Iowa. Colonel Hebard was afterward United States Commissioner to the Paris Exposition in 1889, and died in 1896. Mrs. Hebard died on Nov. 7, 1915, in her 101st year. Her account, written in 1880, is taken from a manuscript in the possession of the Chicago Historical Society.]

Journeying from New London, Connecticut, with my husband and daughter, to our home in Iowa, it was found necessary, as often before, to spend Sunday in Chicago; and all through the weary hours of October 8, 1871, we were enjoying pleasant anticipation of the rest and comfort so sure to be found at the Palmer House [Plate 17]. Arriving late, and leaving most of our baggage at the Union Depot [Plate 18], we were soon established at the hotel, which seemed almost like a home to us. The wind was high on Sunday morning, and kept increasing; and as we walked to church, covering our faces from the dust, my husband remarked, "How fortunate that the fire was last night instead of today."

Returning from an evening service, we were told that another fire had broken out in the western part of the city and was progressing rapidly. We immediately took the elevator to the upper story of the Palmer, saw the fire, but, deciding that it would not cross the river, descended to our rooms in the second story to prepare for sleep. Husband and daughter soon retired; I remained up to prepare for the morrow's journey, and thus gain a little time for shopping before the departure of the train at 11 A.M. Feeling somewhat uneasy, I frequently opened the blinds, and each time found the light in the streets increased until every spire and dome seemed illuminated. I aroused my husband, asking him to go out and investigate once more, which he did, telling me, on his return, not to be alarmed, as there was no danger in our locality.

About 11 P.M. I retired, but could not sleep, and it seemed not more than half an hour before there was a rapping at every door, and finally at ours, to which my husband responded very coolly, "What's wanted?" "Fire, sir!" was the answer, and the same moment we were on our feet. Our daughter was awakened, toilets soon made, and no time wasted in gathering together bags and shawls ready for departure. By this time my husband, who had stepped out

to reconnoiter, returned, saying that everyone was stirring, and that he saw gentlemen dragging their own trunks down the stairs. The clerks at the office assured him there was no immediate danger, but they thought it well enough to be prepared. Then we all went once more to the seventh story, looked in vain for any evidence that the fire was decreasing, returned to our room, picked up our parcels, including the trunk (for no porters were to be found), descended to the office, paid our bill, and sat down to watch and wait. Finally, leaving our daughter in charge of the baggage, I went with my husband into the street, and around to the rear of the building where the fire was distinctly visible and apparently only two blocks from us.

Within the house the perfect quiet had astonished us—every man taking care of his own, silently and rapidly, few words being spoken; only some ladies unaccompanied by gentlemen consulting together in whispers what they should do if compelled to leave the house. Outside we found confusion. Irish women with beds upon their shoulders crying noisily; children following as best they might; and all going—they knew not whither—only away from their burning homes.

Evidently the Palmer House was in great danger, and it was better to leave it now than to wait; but how to remove our baggage was the next question. Once we thought we had secured a cart or a wagon, but no sooner was the trunk thrown on than it was pulled off again by someone claiming a prior right, and we were glad to accept the services of two boys, who, for sufficient compensation, agreed to carry it between them; and thus we sallied forth, a little before 1 A.M., to reach, if possible, the house of my relative, Mr. G. S. Hubbard, on La Salle Street, a long mile and a half from the hotel. Our boys ran at full speed, and we followed, crossing State Street bridge amid a shower of coals driven by the furious wind from burning buildings and lumberyards, and

Plate 17. *The Palmer House, Potter Palmer's palatial hotel at State and Quincy Streets, was completed just before the Great Fire. (Courtesy of the Chicago Historical Society)*

which, seeming to be caught by an eddy, were whirled in our faces.

The crowd thickened every moment; women with babies and bundles, men with kegs of beer—all jostling, scolding, crying, or swearing; and we were thankful to turn from this great thoroughfare to a more quiet street, calling to the boys to slacken their speed and give us a chance to breathe. It must have been 1:30 A.M. when we reached Mr. Hubbard's, thankful that we had, as we supposed, found a place of safety. We dismissed our boys with $10 for their services, and, ringing for admittance, were met at the door by our friends, who were all astir—less on account of apprehension for their own safety than a desire to help others. Soon other friends of the family

began to arrive, some already homeless, until the rooms were filled.

The fire, meanwhile, was coming nearer, and just as we began in earnest to pack necessary things for removal, the Gasworks were destroyed and candles had to be resorted to. Everyone thought the house might be saved, standing as it did on a corner and disconnected from every other building, but we worked on through the night, preparing for the worst, and running often to the garret to see if the worst was not over.

In the early morning men came, tore up carpets to cover the roof, draining both cisterns to keep the

Plate 18. *The ruins of the Central Union Passenger Depot, typical of the devastation wrought by the fire on Chicago's rail transportation. (Photograph by Jex Bardwell, courtesy of the Chicago Historical Society)*

CORNER
STATE & MADISON ST
AFTER CHICAGO FIRE

Plate 19. The destroyed heart of the city at State and Madison Streets, three blocks from the Palmer House. (Courtesy of the Chicago Historical Society)

carpets wet, hoping if possible to stop the fire at that corner. Oh, how they worked! The thoughtful family provided refreshments as long as it was possible, and when all supplies were exhausted the men labored on, panting and parched with thirst, drinking the very dregs of the cistern water from tubs in the kitchen as they passed through. All said, "This house will not burn!" but they might as well have tried to quench Vesuvius. The heat increased. A wooden block nearby flashed into flame, and at 11 A.M. the cornice was blazing, and we were obliged to go out through the alley to escape the heat and cinders; but where to go we could not tell.

From this point it is impossible for me to describe the course of our wanderings. I only know that we crossed to the west side of the river and reached some depot—I think the Northwestern—in season to see the train departing, but hearing that a train on the Chicago, Burlington & Quincy Railroad would leave about 3 P.M., we again set forth.

It was a weary march of many miles after leaving La Salle Street. Exhausted and footsore, we often sat on doorsteps and curbstones to rest; drank beer at the street corners; dropped to sleep while waiting to be served; and finally, at a little station in the outskirts of the city, in company with other refugees like ourselves, we patiently waited for the departure of the train for Aurora, where we passed the night. Strange to say, we lost nothing by the fire—the baggage at the Union Depot was all moved and protected; the few things at Mr. Hubbard's house were not stolen, like some of theirs, but were carefully restored to us.

And now, looking back after the lapse of nine years the whole scene seems like a fearful dream; and yet, strange as it may seem, there are some pleasant things to be remembered; and since it was to be, I have never regretted that we were allowed to see that burning city [Plate 19]. Having nothing of our own at stake, we could perhaps look on more coolly than some others. I remember being impressed at the time with the different phases of character so suddenly unveiled. The dear friends who so kindly sheltered us in our extremity, and who, for the last time, threw open those hospitable doors, not to friends merely, but to strangers as well—feeding the hungry, helping and sympathizing with those whose trials seemed greater than they could bear; those friends who looked on calmly as the devouring flames approached their beautiful dwelling, showing plainly that their treasure was laid up in a better country, where they looked for "a house not made with hands." Some came there, trembling and fearful, wholly broken-down, as it were, with their own grief; some came professedly to help—really to pilfer; but the majority were calm, earnest, resolute helpers; and if ready hands and willing feet could have availed anything, that house would have been saved. As it is, we are thankful that lives were spared, new comforts provided, and faith strengthened in Him who said, "Not as the world giveth, give I unto you."

H. W. S. Cleveland

[Cleveland was appointed landscape architect of the South Park Board in 1872, and was responsible in a large measure for the development of that system. His account is taken from a manuscript, dated November 10, 1871, in the possession of the Chicago Historical Society.]

While the events of the Great Fire are still fresh in my memory I wish to record my personal experiences and observations for future reference if required. They are necessarily confined within narrow limits, as my efforts to save my own property made it impossible to pay other than incidental attention to the scenes around me, yet the simple narrative of what I did and saw may hereafter possess interest.

I was at the time, and am still, boarding with my wife at 883 Indiana Avenue, S.E. corner of 18th Street, which is more than a mile from the nearest point of the burnt district; and it seems now that our being at this place was almost a special dispensation, as we had moved here only the Monday previous from No. 284 Wabash Avenue, three doors south of Van Buren Street, which house was consumed. . . . Moreover, before coming here we had seriously thought of taking a house on the North Side, as some of our friends there were urgent we should do, where we should most certainly have lost everything we had.

My wife's sister, Mrs. Bruce, of Bangor, was with us, having been some weeks in the city—her first visit to us.

On the night of Saturday, October 7th, there was a great fire on the West Side, of which we saw the light; and on Sunday morning I took my early walk to the ruins, and brought back the Sunday *Tribune* containing an account of the "Great Fire," and at breakfast we were discussing it as a terrible calamity, little dreaming how soon it would sink into insignificance in comparison with the destruction which followed.

On Sunday night when we went to bed, before ten o'clock, another alarm had been sounded, and we could see by the bright light in the west that another fire was raging, and from the direction we thought it must have broken out anew from the ruins of the night before. It was evidently distant, and as the scenes at a fire have little attraction for me I felt no inclination to go to it, and we went to bed at the usual hour.

About two o'clock Monday morning we were awakened by my son Ralph, who knocked at the door

to tell us that Mr. Thayer, with whom we boarded, had come from the fire to rouse the family to come and see it, as it had got beyond the control of the firemen and was sweeping everything before it. My wife summoned her sister, but before we were ready Ralph went off with Mr. Thayer and his family.

We went down Wabash Avenue, the streets being lighted by the glare so that we could see people several blocks from us. We supposed on starting that the fire was on the West Side, and meant to go west on Twelfth Street, but before we got there we learned that it had crossed the river, and we therefore kept on down Wabash Avenue, which was rapidly becoming thronged with people. My wife began presently to urge me to leave her and Mrs. Bruce, and to go to my office, which she thought must be in danger; but I could not believe it possible the fire could make its way through such a compact mass of brick and stone as it would have to encounter before reaching my office, which was in the third story of the Shepard Building at the southeast corner of Dearborn and Monroe streets [Plate 20].

By the time we got to Hubbard Court, however, my own apprehensions were aroused, and as the streets were as light as day and thronged with people, I felt no hesitation in leaving the ladies. They seated themselves on the steps of the church at the corner of the Court, and I went on to Monroe, and then west to Dearborn.

The fire had then reached La Salle Street, two blocks from Dearborn, and was surging on like a sea. It was obvious that there was scarcely a chance that the Shepard Building could be saved. I went in at the Monroe Street entrance, and on going into my office, which was as light as day from the glare of the fire, the first thing my eye lighted on was my shawl rolled and strapped as I had left it on my return on Saturday from Indianapolis.

This made me think of my Maynard rifle, which I am accustomed in traveling to carry rolled in my shawl, and my first act was to open my gun case and take out the stock and the two barrels, and roll and

Plate 20. The Shepard Block, southeast corner of Dearborn and Monroe Streets, was one of the downtown buildings Chicagoans thought of as fireproof. (Private Collection)

strap them in my shawl. I also took the bullet pouch, containing a few cartridges and appendages, and a little *lignum vitae* mallet which my son Henry had turned for me, and which I resolved for his sake to save, and so thrust it into my pocket. Then I opened the drawers and seized a few papers and instruments which I could carry in my pockets, and slinging my shawl over my shoulder hurried back as fast as possible to Hubbard Court, where my wife and Mrs. Bruce were waiting for me. I gave them a roll of plans and Henry's mallet, and as the streets were full of people and light as day there seemed no necessity of my remaining with them; I accordingly left them to make their own way home, and returned to my office to try to save some of its contents.

The streets were thronged with fugitives carrying whatever they could save on their backs or in wagons or wheelbarrows, and, in many instances, dragging trunks by a rope through the handle. But there was little or no confusion, and nothing like a panic. Everybody seemed cool and collected and exerting himself to save his own and others' property, or seeking a good position for observation, and it is a sufficient refutation of the absurd stories which have since been circulated of outrages, lynchings, etc., to state the simple

fact that my wife and her sister after I left them, which was about 3 A.M., were a long time walking about the streets in the vicinity of the fire as mere spectators, and finally returned home before daylight without ever a feeling of insecurity, or receiving an uncivil word from anyone. It must be borne in mind, however, that they were to windward of the fire, and of course were in no danger from it, and felt nothing of the suffocating smoke and storm and cinders, which carried the fire northward with such fury that those who were to leeward had to fly for their lives.

After leaving my wife, I deposited my shawl, with my rifle in it, at a friend's house, corner of Wabash Avenue and Harrison Street, and then hurried back to my office. I ought to mention that Mr. S. S. Greeley, City Surveyor, had his office connecting with mine, but as he lived on the North Side he had all he could do to save the lives of his family, and of course made no attempt to reach his office —which indeed would have been impossible.

I had hardly entered my office and begun getting together my most valuable articles when Mr. Greeley's clerk, John Newman, came in and told me that he had already removed the most valuable papers from the safe, and carried them, with Mr. Greeley's notebooks, to the corner of State Street, where a friend of his was watching them while he came back for more.

I then got together all my account books and papers of value, including two large scrapbooks in which I had preserved all my published communications to newspapers, periodicals, etc., for twenty years past. These I wrapped in strong paper and tied them up, helped Newman do up various packages, and then shouldering my transit, which was a very valuable instrument, and as much else as I could carry, we went down to State Street, where we found his friend watching the things he had previously left there.

The wind by this time had increased to a gale from the southwest, and the dust was blinding. We then . . . decided we had better move the things we had saved to a greater distance from the fire, and accordingly carried them all down to Wabash Avenue and placed them on the sidewalk against the wall of the building at the southwest corner. It was a brick building which had been a dwelling house, but was then occupied by various offices, among which was that of Dr. Cushing, dentist, whom we knew. Newman and I then went back to the Shepard Building, and while he was getting together various things of Mr. Greeley's, I took from a closet in my office a large box in which were a variety of odds and ends, some of great value to me. . . . In this box I also had several pounds of powder in tin canisters, which I was anxious to get out of the way.

Then I took out an old fustian coat from the closet and put it on over my other, and stuffed the pockets of both full of such things as I could thus carry off, and also took a drawer from my table and filled it with papers, instruments, etc., and tied a big sheet of strong brown paper over it, and finally took my old leather knapsack, stuffed it full of my most valuable books and strapped it on my shoulders. Then, taking my gun case under one arm, and the drawer under the other, Mr. Newman shouldered the big box, and thus we went down to State Street, by which time we were glad to change loads, Newman taking the gun case and drawer while I shouldered the big box, and thus we reached Wabash Avenue and deposited our loads with the property we had previously left there, and which had been guarded in our absence by Newman's friend.

We now thought it no longer prudent to return to the Shepard Building, and indeed it began to be evident that we must remove our things from the point we then occupied, but how to do it we were puzzled to know. We had brought it two squares with much labor, by making several trips. The nearest point we knew at which we could leave it with any certainty of safety was too far off for us, . . . even if we had a clear track; but by this time it was difficult to make one's way through the crowd of people on the sidewalks and of vehicles in the streets, all loaded with articles of every imaginable description, and all endeavoring to make their way against the pitiless, blinding storm of dust which was driven with acutely painful force in our faces.

It was of course almost a hopeless task to attempt to get a cart, but Newman thought he might possibly find an express man whom he knew, and who, he was confident, would help us if he could. He accordingly set off in search of him, while I remained to watch the property. While he was gone I set myself to rearranging them in more compact and portable form. First I took from my knapsack some articles of little worth and threw them away, and put others in their places. In doing this I found some stout cord, with which I again tied up the bundles of note and account books . . . Then I rearranged my gun case, and stuffed in papers and whatever would go there, and finally piled them all up in such position that they could be easily seized for removal. Then I could do nothing but wait and watch the scenes around me.

Looking west on Monroe Steet from Wabash Avenue, I could see that the Honoré Block and the Post Office, on the southwest and northwest corners of Dearborn were in flames [Plates 21–23], but could not make out whether the Shepard Building was yet on fire. The nearest point of the fire was the Palmer House, corner of State and Quincy streets, which was all in flames. Looking north on Wabash Avenue, I could see that it was all burning on the east side, north of Randolph Street, but had not yet got to the south of Randolph.

Plate 21. The Honoré Block, at the northwest corner of Dearborn and Adams Streets, another so-called fireproof structure, as it appeared after the Great Fire. (Courtesy of the Chicago Historical Society)

The sidewalks as far as I could see were piled up with goods, which had been brought out from stores and houses to be ready for removal if opportunity offered [Plate 24]. A poor Irish woman with a baby asleep in her arms sat upon the sidewalk close by my pile, with her back against the wall. She looked very anxious, but was perfectly quiet, till a rough-looking fellow came up with a bottle of whiskey in his hand, the neck of which he broke off against the wall, and then proceeded to dispose of the contents with three or four companions, drinking from the broken bottle. Some of the whiskey was spilled upon the head of the child, and the woman looked up with an exclamation of impatience at his brutality. I thought by the looks of the men that they might give me some trouble, but they went off without other evidence of ruffianism

ABOVE: *Plate 22. The Chicago Post Office and Customhouse, Dearborn and Monroe Streets, as it looked about 1869. (Courtesy of the Chicago Historical Society)* LEFT: *Plate 23. The interior of the Post Office and Customhouse after the fire. (Courtesy of the Chicago Historical Society)* OPPOSITE: *Plate 24. Refugees from the flames living in the streets.* (Harper's Weekly, October 28, 1871)

than profanity; and this was the only instance in which I saw or heard any sign of brutality.

Soon after a horse came tearing down the avenue, with the wreck of a buggy at his heels, and I fully expected that serious mischief would ensue; but he made his way by some means through the crowd and disappeared without doing any injury that I could see. This was the only runaway I saw; and I was continually surprised at the sober, matter-of-fact way in which the horses did their work, showing no sign of alarm, notwithstanding the appearance of the streets was wholly unlike what they were accustomed to.

It must have been at least an hour and a half that I remained watching the goods before I saw anyone I knew, and the first one was Newman's friend, who had previously watched them. He came up with a smiling face to tell me that the Shepard Building was past danger, which seemed to me so absurd that I at first thought he was joking, and when he insisted on it, I set him down for a fool. Presently Newman appeared, and confirmed the story, which I still could not believe, though he assured me the occupants of many of the offices were carrying their things back to the rooms from which they had been taken. The crowds of people and piles of goods in the streets rendered it idle to attempt to get our things back to the office, and, on examining the situation, we decided to deposit them in Dr. Cushing's office.

The volumes of smoke prevented our seeing any considerable distance, but Newman assured me that the Honoré Building and Bigelow Hotel, which were on the opposite side of Dearborn Street from the Shepard Building (between Monroe and Adams streets), were both destroyed; and as the Shepard was the only building on the east side in that block there was no longer any danger except from such cinders as might come from the ruins, as nothing else was left on the windward side.

On State Street the Palmer House, at the corner of Quincy Street, was burned; but so far as we could see to the south the fire had not crossed to the east side of State Street. The foundations only had been built of the new Palmer House at the corner of Monroe and State, and it seemed, therefore, that there was scarcely a chance that the fire could reach the point where I had so long mounted guard over our goods, so, with the permission of the janitor, we put the whole of them in the back room, piling them carefully by themselves, and then started for the Shepard Building, little thinking we had taken our last look at them.

Making our way through the crowd, we entered the Shepard Building at the north end on Monroe Street, and on going to my office found Ralph quietly looking out of the window at the ruins of the Honoré Building opposite, a large portion of the front wall of which fell into the street at that moment.

Ralph told me that on first starting out he went over to the West Side, and skirting to the windward of the fire, went north to Kinzie Street, where he crossed the bridge to the North Side, intending to cross the main river at State or Rush Street, and so come up to the office. He went as far east as Dearborn Street; finding that the bridges were burned, and the fire running with fearful rapidity, he retraced his steps to the West Side, and then had to go south to Twelfth Street before he could cross the river. He then made his way to the Shepard Building, through Third Avenue.

When he reached Jackson Street, the Bigelow Hotel and Honoré Building were both in flames [Plate 25]; and he covered his face and ran down the opposite side of the street to the Shepard Building, where, finding that we had carried off the things of most value, he went to work and took down the large photographs of Sarah's house from the walls, together with a fine pair of deer's horns, and my English bow and arrows which hung over them. He took all our plans (over two hundred) from the drawers, and rolled them up, and tied them with the cords which he took from the pictures, carried them down, and left them with a pile of furniture which a woman was watching on the sidewalk, and came back to the office, where we found him.

On examining the situation, I saw no reason to doubt the safety of the building. The Post Office, which was the diagonally opposite corner, the Honoré Building directly opposite, and the Bigelow Hotel a little farther south, were all destroyed; and immediately south, on our side of the street, was a vacant lot of half a square. Nothing was left to windward of us but ruins, and though the air was hot that came from them, there seemed little chance that the fire could now reach us. It seemed so incredible, and gave me so much the feeling of a reprieved criminal that I could hardly trust my senses; but the occupants of other offices in the building were busily at work bringing back the things they had carried away, and no one doubted that the danger was past; so, after mutual expressions of congratulation, I unstrapped my knapsack, which I had not previously taken from my shoulders, took off my old coat with its pockets full of valuables, and, leaving them on our case of drawers, went with Ralph and brought up the things he had carried down.

It was now about 7 A.M., and knowing how anxious my wife would be to hear from us, and feeling sure that I had good news to tell, I left Ralph and Newman in the office, and started for home. Remembering, however, that Mr. Thayer's office was in the *Tribune* Building (corner Dearborn and Madison), and wishing to assure myself of its safety by actual inspection, I made my way along Dearborn to

Plate 25. The grand entrance of the Bigelow House on Dearborn Street next to the Honoré Block. The hotel was preparing to open when the fire struck. (Photograph by Jex Bardwell, courtesy of the Chicago Historical Society)

Madison (the west side of Dearborn being all burned), and so down Madison to Wabash Avenue, and then home. The *Tribune* Building was then unharmed, and I supposed was past danger.

I found my family just sitting down to breakfast, which was eaten with lighter hearts for the good news I brought. Nobody knew anything about the condition of the North Side, though the opinion was unanimous that it must be swept clean if the fire crossed the river. There was a rumor that the Waterworks were destroyed and the whole North Side, but no one could tell what was truth and what was rumor.

After breakfast I prepared to return, and found that the fire was raging on the north side of Harrison Street, between Wabash Avenue and State Street, and on both sides of the Avenue as far as I could see. I went to try to ascertain the fate of the Shepard Building. As I could not go through Harrison Street on account of the fire, I went south to Peck Court, and then west, through Polk Street, to Third Avenue. Tried there to go north, but could not go beyond Harrison. I managed to go one square west on Harrison to Fourth Avenue, which was burnt so clean on both sides that I could traverse it without difficulty, except that the smoke and hot air were at times very disagreeble. I could see but a little way. I reached Van Buren Street, and then went east to Third Avenue, as Fourth was too fiery to admit further passage.

On Van Buren Street, I first saw the effect of the fire on the wooden pavements, which in places had been burned in alternate little ridges and gutters not more than half an inch in depth. The pavement had nowhere sustained any serious injury, and much of it was not even scorched.

From Van Buren Street I went through Third Avenue and Adams Street to Dearborn; and it was not till I reached that point that I could see that nothing remained of the Shepard Building but some fragments of the walls. I could go no farther, and started back through Third Avenue. I presently met two men who asked me if they could get through, and seemed to think I had come from unknown depths of the furnace before them. These were the only living beings I saw from the time I entered the burned district till I emerged again on Harrison Street, and the solitude seemed to render the desolation more impressive.

Ralph made his appearance at dinner time, and reported that, after I left them, he and Newman stationed themselves at a window at the south end of the building to watch for cinders, as it was only from that quarter they apprehended danger. But it seems that the fire crept upon them unawares from the leeward side, and the first they knew of its approach was seeing flames darting through the windows at the northern end. They could not even get down the stairs at that end, but had barely time to run into the office, where Ralph seized a roll of plans, and he and Newman together took a trunk between them, and ran down and out at the door on Dearborn Street, and then across the street to the alley behind the walls of the Post Office, where they were kept prisoners, and half suffocated with the smoke and heat for nearly two hours before they could make their escape, which they finally did by covering their faces and running out through Monroe and Clark streets, leaving the things they had saved, which they recovered some hours afterward.

Horace White

[The account of Horace White (Plate 26), editor-in-chief of the *Chicago Tribune*, was written as a letter to Murat Halstead, who published it in the *Cincinnati Commercial*, of which he was editor, in October 1871.]

As a slight acknowledgment of your thoughtful kindness in forwarding to us, without orders, a complete outfit of type and cases, when you heard that we had been burned out, I send you a hastily written sketch of what I saw at the Great Fire . . .

The history of the Great Fire in Chicago, which rises to the dignity of a national event, cannot be written until each witness, who makes any record whatever, shall have told what he saw. Nobody could see it all—no more than one man could see the whole of the Battle of Gettysburg. It was too vast, too swift, too full of smoke, too full of danger, for anybody to see it all. My experience derives its only public importance from the fact that what I did, substantially, a hundred thousand others did or attempted—that is, saved, or sought to save, their lives and enough of their wearing apparel to face the sky in. As you have printed in your columns a map of the burned district [Plate 27], I will remark that my starting point was at my residence, No. 148 Michigan Avenue, between Monroe and Adams streets.

What I saw at the Great Fire embraces nothing more heartrending than the destruction of property. I saw no human beings burned or suffocated in flame and smoke, though there were many. My brother early in the fray stumbled over the bodies of two dead men near the corner of La Salle and Adams streets. My wife saw the body of a dead boy in our own dooryard as she was taking leave of our home. How it got there we know not. Probably it was brought there as to a place of safety, the bearers leaving and forgetting it, or themselves getting fast in some inextricable throng of fugitives. I saw no mothers with newborn babes hurried into the street and carried miles through the night air by the light of burning houses. I have a friend whose wife gave birth to a child within one hour of the time when the flames of Sunday night reddened the sky. Her home was in the North Division which was swept clean of some ten thousand houses. This suffering lady was taken downstairs with her infant, and carried one mile to a place of supposed safety. She had not been there an hour when she was taken out a second time and carried a mile

Plate 26. *Horace White, who was editor-in-chief of the* Chicago Tribune *from 1865 to 1875. (Courtesy of the Chicago Historical Society)*

and a half westward. Blessed be God that she still lives and that the young child breathes sweetly on her bosom!

I had retired to rest, though not to sleep [Sunday, October 8], when the great bell struck the alarm; but fires had been so frequent of late, and had been so speedily extinguished, that I did not deem it worthwhile to get up and look at it, or even to count the strokes of the bell to learn where it was. The bell paused for fifteen minutes before giving the general alarm, which distinguishes a great fire from a small

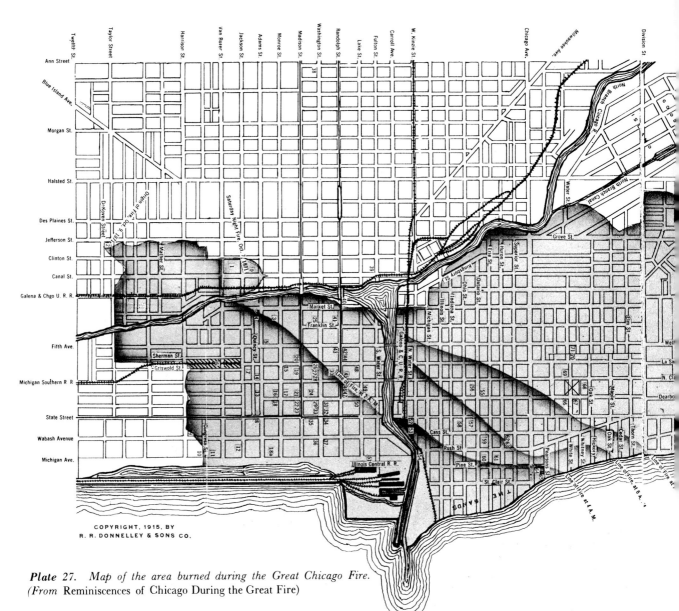

*Plate 27. Map of the area burned during the Great Chicago Fire.
(From Reminiscences of Chicago During the Great Fire)*

KEY TO MAP

0 Saturday Night Fire
1 Lull & Holmes's Planing Mill
2 Home of Mrs. Patrick O'Leary
3 Gasworks
4 Armory
5 Conley's Patch
6 Michigan Southern Depot
7 Grand Pacific Hotel
8 Palmer House
9 Wabash Ave. Methodist Church
10 Michigan Ave. Hotel
11 Terrace Row
12 Trinity Church
13 Bigelow Hotel
14 Lakeside Publishing Co.
15 Nixon Building
16 Honoré Block
17 Post Office. Customhouse
18 Shepard Building

18a Horace White Residence
19 Farwell Hall
20 Otis Block
21 Reynolds Block
22 Tribune Building
23 McVicker's Theatre
24 Times Building
25 Nevada Hotel
26 Chamber of Commerce
27 Brunswick Hall
28 Methodist Church
29 Portland Block
30 Courthouse
31 Crosby's Opera House
32 St. James Hotel
33 First National Bank
34 Field, Leiter & Co.
35 Booksellers' Row
36 Drake-Farwell Block

37 Second Presbyterian Church
38 First Congregational Church
39 Avery's Lumber Yard
40 Lind Block
41 Schuttler Wagon Factory
42 Briggs House
43 Metropolitan Hotel
44 Metropolitan Block
45 Sherman House
46 Wood's Museum
47 Matteson House
48 Marine Bank
49 Shay's Dry Goods Store
50 Tremont House
51 Illinois Central R.R. Land Dept.
52 Wright Bros. Livery Stable
53 Galena Elevator
54 McCormick Reaper Factory
55 Chicago Historical Society

56 Robt. A. Kinzie Residence
57 Haines H. Magie Residence
58 Lambert Tree Residence
59 William B. Ogden Residence
60 Walter L. Newberry Residence
61 Isaac N. Arnold Residence
62 Julian S. Rumsey Residence
63 George F. Rumsey Residence
64 Waterworks
65 Lill's Brewery
66 New England Congregational
   Church
67 Unity Church
68 Mahlon D. Ogden Residence
69 Ezra B. McCagg Residence
70 Gurdon S. Hubbard Residence
71 David Fales Residence
72 Dr. J. H. Foster Residence

Plate 28. *The* Chicago Tribune *building at the corner of Dearborn and Madison Streets shortly before the fire.* (Harper's Weekly, *October 28, 1871*).

one. When it sounded the general alarm I rose and looked out. There was a great light to the southwest of my residence, but no greater than I had frequently seen in that quarter, where vast piles of pine lumber have been stored all the time I have lived in Chicago, some eighteen years. But it was not pine lumber that was burning this time. It was a row of wooden tenements in the South Division of the city in which a few days ago were standing whole rows of the most costly buildings which it hath entered into the hearts of architects to conceive. I watched the increasing light a few moments. Red tongues of light began to shoot upward; my family were all aroused by this time, and I dressed myself for the purpose of going to the *Tribune* office to write something about the catastrophe. Once out upon the street, the magnitude of the fire was suddenly disclosed to me.

The dogs of hell were upon the housetops of La Salle and Wells streets, just south of Adams, bounding from one to another. The fire was moving nothward like ocean surf on a sand beach. It had already traveled an eighth of a mile and was far beyond control. A column of flame would shoot up from a burning building, catch the force of the wind, and

strike the next one, which in turn would perform the same direful office for its neighbor. It was simply indescribable in its terrible grandeur. Vice and crime had got the first scorching. The district where the fire got its first firm foothold was the Alsatia of Chicago. Fleeing before it was a crowd of blear-eyed, drunken, and diseased wretches, male and female, half naked, ghastly, with painted cheeks, cursing and uttering ribald jests as they drifted along.

I went to the *Tribune* office [Plates 28 and 29], ascended to the editorial rooms, took the only inflammable thing there, a kerosene lamp, and carried it to the basement, where I emptied the oil into the sewer. This was scarcely done when I perceived the flames breaking out of the roof of the Courthouse, the old nucleus of which, in the center of the edifice, was not constructed of fireproof material, as the new wings had been. As the flames had leaped a vacant space of nearly two hundred feet to get at this roof, it was evident that most of the business portion of the city must go down; but I did not reflect that the city Waterworks, with their four great pumping engines, were in a straight line with the fire and wind. Nor did I know then that this priceless machinery was covered by a wooden roof. The flames were driving thither with demon precision.

What happened at the *Tribune* Building has already been told in your columns. We saw the tall buildings on the opposite sides of the two streets melt down in a few moments without scorching ours. The heat broke the plate-glass windows in the lower stories, but not in the upper ones. After the fire in our neighborhood had spent its force, the editorial and composing rooms did not even smell of smoke. Several of our brave fellows who had been up all night had gone to sleep on the lounges while others were at the sink washing their faces, supposing that all danger to us had passed. So I supposed, and in this belief went home to breakfast. The smoke to the northward was so dense that we could not see the North Division, where sixty thousand people were flying in mortal terror before the flames. The immense store of Field, Leiter & Co. [Plates 30 and 31] I observed to be under a shower of water from their own fire apparatus, and since the First National Bank [Plates 32 and 33], a fireproof building, protected it on one corner, I concluded that the progress of the flames in that direction was stopped, as the *Tribune* Building had stopped it where we were. Here, at least, I thought was a saving of twenty millions of property, including the Great Central Depot and the two grain elevators adjoining [Plates 34–36], effected by two or three buildings which had been erected with a view to such an emergency. The Post Office and Customhouse building (also fireproof according to public rumor) had stopped the flames a little farther to the southwest, although the interior of that structure was burning. A straight line drawn northeast from the Post Office would nearly touch the *Tribune*, First National Bank, Field, Leiter & Co.'s store, and the Illinois Central Railroad land department, another fireproof. Everything east of that line seemed perfectly safe, and with this feeling I went home to breakfast.

With some little difficulty we reached our house, and in less time than we ever set out on a journey before, we dragged seven trunks, four bundles, four valises, two baskets, and one hamper of provisions into the street and piled them on the wagon. The fire was still more than a quarter of a mile distant, and the wind, which was increasing in violence, was driving it not exactly in our direction. The low wooden houses were nearly all gone, and after that the fire must make progress, if at all, against brick and stone. Several churches of massive architecture were between us and harm, and the great Palmer House had not been reached, and might not be if the firemen, who had now got their hose into the lake, could work efficiently in the ever-increasing jam of fugitives.

OPPOSITE: ***Plate 29.*** *The gutted* Tribune *building.* *(Courtesy of the Chicago Historical Society)*

Plate 30. *The splendid white marble store of Field, Leiter & Co., the firm that later became Marshall Field & Co., at the corner of Washington and State Streets before 1871. (Courtesy of the Chicago Historical Society)*

My wife thought we should have time to take another load; my brother thought so; we all thought so. We had not given due credit either to the savage strength of the fire or the firm pack on Michigan Avenue. Leaving my brother to get the family safely out if I did not return in time, and to pile the most valuable portion of my library into the drawers and bureaus and tables ready for moving, I seized a bird

Plate 31. *The remains of the Field, Leiter department store after the flames had swept up State Street. (Courtesy of the Chicago Historical Society)*

ABOVE: *Plate 32.* The First National Bank Building, State and Washington Streets, was one of Chicago's iron-and-stone structures advertised as fireproof. (Courtesy of the Chicago Historical Society) LEFT: *Plate 33.* The First National Bank Building after its fireproof claims had been tested. (Courtesy of the Chicago Historical Society) OPPOSITE, TOP: *Plate 34.* The Illinois and Michigan Central Depot, one of the city's most important rail terminals, as seen from the corner of Madison Street and Michigan Avenue. Lake Michigan is on the right. (From Edwin Whitefield's Views of Chicago, courtesy of the Chicago Historical Society) OPPOSITE, BOTTOM: *Plate 35.* The ruins of the Illinois and Michigan Central Depot with its south wall still standing. (Courtesy of the Chicago Historical Society)

Plate 36. *The grain elevators burn at the mouth of the Chicago River near the Central Depot. Miraculously, some of the largest of the elevators survived.* (Harper's Weekly, November 4, 1871)

cage containing a talented green parrot, and mounted the seat with the driver. For one square southward from the corner of Monroe Street we made pretty fair progress. The dust was so thick that we could not see the distance of a whole square ahead. It came, not in clouds, but in a steady storm of sand, the particles impinging against our faces like needle points. Pretty soon we came to a dead halt. We could move neither forward nor backward, nor sidewise. The gorge had caught fast somewhere. Yet everybody was good-natured and polite. If I should say I didn't hear an oath all the way down Michigan Avenue, there are probably some mule drivers in Cincinnati who would say it was a lie. But I did not. The only quarrelsome person I saw was a German laborer (a noted exception to his race), who was protesting that he had lost everything, and that he would not get out of the middle of the road although he was on foot. He became very obstreperous on this point, and commenced beating the head of my horse with his fist. My driver was preparing to knock him down with the butt end of his whip, when two men seized the insolent Teuton and dragged him to the water's edge, where it is to be hoped he was ducked.

By getting into the park, we succeeded in advancing two squares without impediment, and might have gone farther had we not come upon an excavation which the public authorities had recently made. This drove us back to the avenue, where another battering ram made a gap for us at the intersection of Van Buren Street, the north end of Michigan Terrace. Here the gorge seemed impassable. The difficulty proceeded from teams entering Michigan Avenue from cross streets. Extempore policemen stationed themselves at the crossings, and helped as well as they could, but we were half an hour in passing the Terrace. From this imposing row of residences the millionaires were dragging their trunks and their bundles, and yet there was no panic, no frenzy, no boisterousness, but only the haste which the situation authorized.

There was real danger to life all along the street, but nobody realized it, because the park was ample to hold all the people. None of us asked or thought what would become of those nearest the water if the smoke, and cinders should drive the whole crowd down to the shore, or if the vast bazaar of luggage should itself take fire, as some of it afterwards did. Fortunately for those in the street, there was a limit to the number of teams available in that quarter of the city. The contributions from the cross streets grew less; and we soon began to move on a walk without interruption. Arriving at Eldridge Court, I turned into Wabash Avenue, where the crowd was thinner. Arriving at the house of a friend, who was on the windward side of the fire, I tumbled off my load and started back to get another.

Half way down Michigan Avenue, which was now perceptibly easier to move in, I discovered my family on the sidewalk, with their arms full of light household effects. My wife told me that the house was already burned, that the flames burst out ready-made in the rear hall before she knew that the roof had been scorched, and that one of the servants, who had disobeyed orders in her eagerness to save some article, had got singed, though not burned, in coming out. My wife and mother, and all the rest were begrimed with dirt and smoke, like blackamoors—everybody was. The "bloated aristocrats" all along the street, who supposed they had lost both home and fortune at one sweep, were a sorry but not despairing congregation. They had saved their lives at all events, and they knew that many of their fellow creatures must have lost theirs.

I saw a great many kindly acts done as we moved along. The poor helped the rich, and the rich helped the poor (if anybody could be called rich at such a time) to get on with their loads. I heard of cartmen demanding one hundred and fifty dollars (in hand, of course) for carrying a single load. Very likely it was so, but those cases did not come under my own notice. It did come under my notice that some cartmen worked for whatever the sufferers felt able to pay, and one I knew worked with alacrity for nothing. It takes all sorts of people to make a great fire.

I had paid and discharged my driver after extorting his solemn promise to come back and move me again if the wind should shift to the north—in which event everybody knew that the whole South Division, for a distance of four miles, must perish. We soon arrived at the house of the kind friend on Wabash Avenue, where our trunks and bundles had been deposited. This was south of the line of fire, but this did not satisfy anybody, since we had all seen how resolutely the flames had gone transversely across the direction of the wind. Then came a story from down the street that Sheridan was going to blow up the Wabash Avenue Methodist Church on the corner of Harrison Street. We observed a general scattering away of people from that neighborhood. I was nearly four squares south of the locality, and thought that the missiles wouldn't come so far. We awaited the explosion, but it did not come. By and by we picked up courage to go around two or three blocks and see whether the church had fallen down of its own accord. We perceived that two or three houses in the rear of the edifice had been leveled to the ground, that the church itself was standing, and that the fire was out, in that quarter at least; also, that the line of Harrison Street marked the southern limits of the devastation.

The wind continued to blow fiercely from the southwest, and has not ceased to this hour (Saturday, October 14). But it was liable to change. If it chopped around to the north, the burning embers would be blown back upon the South Division. If it veered to the east, they would be blown into the West Division, though the river afforded rather better protection there. Then we should have nothing to do but to keep ahead of the flames and get down as fast as possible to the open prairie, and there spend the night houseless and supperless—and what of the morrow? A full hundred thousand of us. And if we were spared, and the West Division were driven out upon their prairie (a hundred and fifty thousand according to the Federal census), how would the multitude be fed? If there could be anything more awful than what we had already gone through, it would be what we would certainly go through if the wind should change; for with the embers of this great fire flying about, and no water to fight them, we knew there was not gunpowder enough in Illinois to stop the inevitable conflagration. But this was not all. A well authenticated rumor came up to the city that the prairie was on fire south of Hyde Park, the largest of the southern suburbs.

The grass was as dry as tinder, and so were the leaves in Cottage Grove, a piece of timber several miles square, containing hundreds of residences of the better class, some of them of palatial dimensions. A fire on the prairie, communicating itself to the grove, might cut off the retreat of the one hundred thousand people in the South Division; might invade the South Division itself, and come up under the impulsion of that fierce wind, and where should we all be then? There were three or four bridges leading to the West Division, the only possible avenues of escape—but what were these among so many? And what if the "Commune" should go to work and start incendiary fires while all was yet in confusion? These fiends were improving the daylight by plundering along the street. Before dark the whole male population of the city was organized by spontaneous impulse into a night patrol, with pallid determination to put every incendiary to instant death.

About 5 P.M. I applied to a friend on Wabash Avenue for the use of a team to convey my family and chattels to the southern suburbs, about four miles distant, where my brother happened to own a small cottage, which, up to the present time, nobody could be induced to occupy and pay rent for. My friend replied that his work-teams were engaged hauling water for people to drink. Here was another thing I had not thought of—a great city with no water to drink. Plenty in the lake, to be sure, but none in the city mains or the connecting pipes. Fortunately the extreme western limits were provided with a number of artesian wells, bored for manufacturing establishments. Then there was the river—the horrible, black, stinking river of a few weeks ago, which has since become clear enough for fish to live in, by reason of the deepening of the canal, which draws to the Mississippi a perpetual flow of pure water from Lake

Plate 37. Fleeing northward before the flames, people seek refuge in Lincoln Park, which until recently had been a cemetery. (Harper's Weekly, *November 11, 1871*)

Michigan. With the city Pumping Works stopped, the sewers no longer discharged themselves into the river. So this might be used; and it was. Twenty-four hours had not passed before tens of thousands of people were drinking the water of Chicago River, with no unpleasant taste or effects.

The work-teams of my friend being engaged in hauling water for people who could not get any from

was given. And thus we started again, our hostess pressing a mattress upon us from her store. All the streets leading southward were yet filled with fugitives. Where they all found shelter that night, I know not; but every house seemed to be opened to anybody who desired to enter.

Arrived at our home about dusk; we found in it, as we expected, a cold reception, there being neither stove nor grate, nor fireplace, nor fuel, nor light therein, But I will not dwell upon these things. We really did not mind them, for when we thought of the thousands of men, women, and tender babes huddled together in Lincoln Park, seven miles to the north of us, with no prospect of food, exposed to rain, if it should come, with no canopy but the driving smoke of their homes, we thought how little we had suffered and how much we should be thankful for [Plate 37]. How one feels at a particular time depends much upon how he sees others enjoy themselves. All the eight-hour strikers are possessed of more comfort and leisure than we have, but we do not notice anything of it at all. We have secured a stove, and there are plenty of trees around us, and the ax is mightier than the pen to get one's breakfast ready now.

The prairie fire southwest of Hyde Park we found to have been a veritable fact, but it had been put out by diligent effort [Plate 38]. The ditches cut for drainage in that region during the last two or three years render it very difficult for a fire to spread far. Yet I revolved in my mind a plan of escape in case the fire should break out afresh, surmount the ditches, and get into the grove which surrounded us. I judged that a fire could be discerned from our window fully five miles away, and that before it could reach us we could get upon the new South Park Boulevard, two hundred feet wide, the western side of which has no timber to burn. A mere prairie fire coming up to this graveled driveway would go out, and we should suffer nothing worse than a little smoke. I learned the next day that some of the people on the lake shore east of us constructed rafts and gathered a few household effects in convenient places, to be launched whenever the fire should make its appearance on the prairie. It turned out, from the experience of the North Division groves, that these oak woods would not have burned in any case, the timber containing too much moisture. But we did not then know that.

There was no sleep for us until we heard the welcome sound of rain against our windows. How our hearts did rise in thankfulness to heaven for rain! We thought the poor people in Lincoln Park would rather have the rain on their heads than know that Chicago was exposed to the horror of total conflagration. The wind blew with increasing violence, till our frame house trembled in every rafter. We did not know but it would go over, yet if it would only rain we would stand our ground, for we had no furniture to be

the wells or the river or lake, he placed at my disposal his carriage, horses, and coachman, whom he directed to take me and the ladies to any place we desired to reach. While we were talking, he hailed another gentleman on the street, who owned a large stevedore wagon, and asked him to convey my trunks, etc., to Cottage Grove Avenue, near Forty-third Street, to which request an immediate and most gracious assent

Plate 38. "Scene on the Prairie Monday Night." (Drawing by Alfred R. Waud, courtesy of the Chicago Historical Society)

broken by an overturned house, or to break our bones rolling about the floor. Now and then we looked at the red sky to the north, and satisfied ourselves that the rest of Chicago was not burning. This gave us comfort, but not sleep.

Details of what I saw might be spun out to the crack of doom, but I must draw it to a close. There will, of course, be much curiosity, to know why the fireproof buildings succumbed. . . .

It is ascertained that no stone ever used in the business part of a city is worth a farthing in such a fire. Brick is the only thing which comes out whole, and is ready to try it again. But it is not fair to say that an absolutely fireproof building cannot be erected. I think it can be. At all events, the architects of the world should come here and study. . . .

And what shall I say of the Christ-like charity that has overwhelmed us in our misfortune? All the tears that have been shed in Chicago, except those which have flowed for the dead and maimed, have been called to our eyes by reading that in this great city and that little town, and yonder hamlet, and across the lakes in Canada, and down among our late enemies of the South, and beyond the mountains in Utah and California, and over the water in England, and on the Continent, God's people were working and giving to

save us our affliction. I cannot even write of it, for my eyes fill whenever I think of it

On Wednesday morning the *Tribune* came out with a half sheet containing among other things a notice that an intelligence office had been opened for lost people to report to, and for those who had lost their friends to inquire at. On the following morning we printed two columns of personal items from this intelligence office. Perhaps you have copied them, but I send you a few taken at random:

Mrs. Bush is at 40 Arnold Street. She lost her baby.
Peter Grace lost wife and children; Church, Carpenter and Washington Streets.
Mrs. Tinney lost little girl six years old, Katie, Harrison House.
James Glass lost little boy, Arthur Glass, 342 Hubbard Street.
A little girl, cannot speak her name, at Desplaines Hotel.
The wife and child of Rev. W. A. Jones are missing.
Henry Schneider, baby, in blue poland waist, red skirt, has white hair.

Many of these lost babies were doubtless found; many of these separated families brought together again. What meetings there must have been! But many others have gone over the river, to be found of God, and delivered to their mothers' arms in mansions not made with hands, eternal in the heavens.

William Bross

[An ex-Lieutenant Governor of Illinois, William Bross (Plate 39) was, together with Joseph Medill and Horace White, publisher of the *Chicago Tribune*. His account was dictated to a reporter of the *New York Tribune* upon his arrival from Chicago at the St. Nicholas Hotel, New York, and was published in the paper on October 14, 1871.]

About two o'clock on Monday morning my family and I were aroused by Mrs. Samuel Bowles, wife of the editor and proprietor of *The Springfield Republican*, who happened to be our guest. We had all gone to bed very tired the night before, and had slept so soundly that we were unaware of the conflagration till it had assumed terrible force. My family were very much alarmed at the glare which illuminated the sky and the lake [Plate 40]. I saw that a dreadful disaster was impending over Chicago, and immediately left the house to determine the locality and extent of the fire. I found that it was then a good deal south of my house, and west of the Michigan Southern and Rock Island railroad depots.

I went home considerably reassured in half an hour, and finding my family packing told them that I did not anticipate danger, and requested them to leave it off. But I said, "The result of this night's work will be awful. At least ten thousand people will want breakfast in the morning; you prepare breakfast for one hundred"; this they proceeded to do, but soon became alarmed and recommenced packing. Soon after half-past two o'clock I started for the *Tribune* office, to see if it was in danger. By this time the fire had crossed the south branch of the river, and that portion of the city south of Harrison Street, between Third Avenue and the river, seemed a blaze of fire.

I reached the *Tribune* office, and, seeing no cause for apprehension, did not remain there more than twenty minutes. On leaving the office I proceeded to the Nevada Hotel (which is my property), corner of Washington and Franklin streets. I remained there for an hour, watching the progress of the flames, and contemplating the destruction going on around. The fire had passed east of the hotel, and I hoped that the building was safe; but it soon began to extend in a westerly direction, and the hotel was quickly enveloped in flames. I became seriously alarmed, and ran north on Franklin Street to Randolph, so as to head off the flames and get back to my house, which was on Michigan Avenue, on the shore of the lake.

Plate 39. *William Bross (standing), a former lieutenant governor of Illinois who was associated with Joseph Medill and Horace White in publishing the* Chicago Tribune. *Other members of the Bross family in this 1877 photograph are his father, Moses Bross, and his daughter, Jessie Bross Lloyd, with her son William on her lap. (Courtesy of the Chicago Historical Society)*

My house was a part of almost the last block burned [in Terrace Row[1]].

At this time the fire was the most grandly magnificent scene that one can conceive. The Courthouse, Post Office, Farwell Hall, Tremont House, Sherman

[1] Terrace Row was situated between Van Buren and Congress streets [Plate 41].

Plate 40. The burning of Chicago as seen from Lake Michigan. The effect of the light from the flames against the night sky left an indelible impression on all who saw it. (The Illustrated London News, October 28, 1871)

House, and all the splendid buildings on La Salle and Wells streets were burning with a sublimity of effect which awed me; all the adjectives in the language would fail to convey the intensity of its wonders. Crowds of men, women, and children were huddling away, running first in one direction, then in another, shouting and crying in their terror, and trying to save anything they could lay their hands on, no matter how trivial in value; while every now and then explosions, which seemed almost to shake the solid earth, would reverberate through the air and add to the terrors of the poor people [Plate 42].

I crossed Lake Street bridge to the west, ran north to Kinzie Street bridge, and crossed over east to the North Side, hoping to head off the fire. It had, however, already swept north of me, and was traveling faster than I could go, and I soon came to the conclusion that it would be impossible for me to get east in that direction. I accordingly re-crossed Kinzie

Street bridge, and went west as far as Des Plaines Street, where I fortunately met a gentleman in a buggy, who very kindly drove me over Twelfth Street bridge, to my house on Michigan Avenue. It was by this time getting on toward five o'clock, and the day was beginning to break. On my arrival home I found my horses already harnessed, and my riding horse saddled for me. My family and friends were busily engaged in packing, and in distributing sandwiches and coffee to all who wanted them, or could spare a minute to partake of them.

I immediately jumped on my horse, and rode as fast as I could to the *Tribune* office. I found everything safe; the men were all there, and we fondly hoped that all danger was past as far as we were concerned—and for this reason: the blocks in front of the *Tribune* Building on Dearborn Street, and north on Madison Street, had both been burned, the only damage accruing to us being confined to a cracking of some of the plate-glass windows from the heat. But a somewhat curious incident soon set us all in a state of excitement. The fire had, unknown to us, crawled under the sidewalk from the wooden pavement and caught the woodwork of the barber's shop which comprised a

Plate 41. *These luxurious private residences situated on Michigan Avenue between Van Buren and Congress Streets were known collectively as Terrace Row and counted among their occupants families such as the Brosses. They were destroyed in the fire. (Courtesy of the Chicago Historical Society)*

portion of our basement. As soon as we ascertained the extent of the mischief, we no longer apprehended any special danger, believing, as we did, that the building was fireproof.

My associates, Mr. Medill and Mr. White, were present, and, with the help of some of our employees we went to work with water and one of Babcock's fire extinguishers. The fire was soon put out, and we once more returned to business. The forms had been sent downstairs, and I ordered our foreman, Mr. Kahler, to get all the pressmen together, in order to issue the paper as soon as a paragraph showing how far the

fire had then extended could be prepared and inserted. Many kind friends gathered around the office and warmly expressed their gratification at the preservation of our building.

Believing all things safe, I again mounted my horse and rode south on State Street to see what progress the fire was making, and if it were moving eastward on Dearborn Street. To my great surprise and horror I found that its current had taken an easterly direction, nearly as far as State Street, and that it was also advancing in a northerly direction with terrible swiftness and power. I saw the danger so imminently threatening us, and with some friends endeavored to obtain a quantity of powder for the purpose of blowing up buildings south of the Palmer House. Failing in finding any powder, I saw the only thing to do was to tear them down.

I proceeded to Church's hardware store, procured

Plate 42. "Fleeing the Burning City." (Drawing by Alfred R. Waud, courtesy of the Chicago Historical Society)

about a dozen heavy axes, and handing them to my friends, requested them to mount the buildings with me and literally chop them down. All but two or three seemed utterly paralyzed at this unexpected change in the course of the fire; and even these, seeing the others stand back, were unwilling to make the effort alone. At this moment I saw that some wooden buildings and a new brick house west of the Palmer House had already caught fire. I knew at a glance that the *Tribune* Building was doomed, and I rode back to the office and told them that nothing more could be done to save the building, McVicker's Theatre, or anything else in that vicinity. In this hopeless frame of mind I rode home to look after my residence and family, intently watching the ominous eastward movement of the flames. I set to work, with my family and friends, to move as much of my furniture as possible across the narrow park east of Michigan Avenue, onto the shore of the lake, a distance of some three hundred feet.

Following out the idea that each citizen should give the incidents happening to himself or under his own observation, I mention that never did friends toil more loyally than ours did for us. They saved most of our books, furniture, pictures, etc., that were left to us. Some that were not friends helped themselves to whatever struck their fancy when opportunity offered.

My coachman filled my buggy with some harness, a bag of coffee, and other articles, and left it with his friends on the lake shore. Someone coming along and finding it was my "plunder," said he knew me; would put some more goods in it to take home, and return the buggy to me. That was the last I ever heard of the buggy or anything that was in it. My daughter suppose that I had hired an express wagon that stood at the door, and I supposed that she had. We filled it full of goods and furniture; among other things, a valuable picture—a farm and animal scene—by Herring, the great English painter. The driver slipped off in the crowd, and that was the last we heard of that picture or any part of the load. I met a man at my door looking decidedly corpulent. "My friend," said I, "you have on a considerable invoice of my clothes, with the hunting suit outside. Well, go along, you might as well have them as to let them burn." These were slight affairs compared with what many others suffered by the thieving crowd.

I sent my family to the house of some friends in the south part of the city for safety; my daughter, Miss Jessie Bross, was the last to leave us.

The work of carrying the furniture across the Avenue to the shore was most difficult and dangerous. For six or eight hours Michigan Avenue was jammed with every description of vehicle, containing families escaping from the city, or baggage wagons laden with goods and furniture. The sidewalks were crowded with men, women, and children, all carrying something. Some of the things saved and carried away were valueless. One woman carrying an empty bird cage; another, an old workbox; another, some dirty, empty baskets. Old, useless bedding, anything that could be hurriedly snatched up, seemed to have been carried away without judgment or forethought.

In the meantime the fire had lapped up the Palmer House, the theatres, and the *Tribune* Building; and contrary to our expectations, for we thought the current of fire had passed my residence, judging from the direction of the wind, we saw, by the advancing clouds of dense black smoke and rapidly approaching flames, that we were in imminent peril.

The fire had already worked so far south and east as to attack the stables in the rear of Terrace Row, between Van Buren and Congress streets. Many friends rushed into the houses in the block, and helped to carry out heavy furniture, such as pianos and bookcases. We succeeded in carrying the bulk of it to the shore. There I sat with a few others by our household goods, calmly awaiting the destruction of our property—one of the most splendid blocks in Chicago. The eleven fine houses, which composed the block, were occupied by Denton Gurney, Peter L. Yoe, Mrs. Humphreys (owned by Mrs. Walker), William Bross, P. F. W. Peck, S. C. Griggs, Tuthill King, Judge H. T. Dickey, Isaac Cook, John L. Clark, and the Hon. J. Y. Scammon.

Having got out all we could about 11 A.M. of Monday, the 9th, I sat down by my goods, which were piled up indiscriminately on the lake shore. Soon I saw the angry flame bursting from my home. Quickly and grandly they wrapped up the whole block, and away it floated in black clouds over Lake Michigan.

Early in the afternoon we began to send our goods south by teams, and by sundown all that we had been able to save was distributed among friends south of Twelfth Street. In the evening my little family of three came together at the house of E. L. Jansen, No. 607 Wabash Avenue, Mrs. Bross's brother, where we remained until most kindly received by Dr. Edmund Andrews and family. There was very little sleep that (Monday) night, for everybody was in mortal fear that what remained of the city would be burned by the desperados who were known to be prowling about everywhere.

The next morning I was out early, and found the streets thronged with people moving in all directions. To me the sight of the ruin, though so sad, was wonderful—giving one a most peculiar sensation, as it

Plate 43. *The impressive ruins of the Grand Pacific Hotel, Clark and Jackson Streets, a brand-new hostelry which was devoured by the fire. (Photograph by Jex Bardwell, courtesy of the Chicago Historical Society)*

was wrought in so short a space of time. It was the destruction of the entire business portion of one of the greatest cities in the world! Every bank and insurance office, law offices, hotels, theatres, railroad depots, most of the churches, and many of the principal residences of the city, a charred mass—property almost beyond estimate gone [Plates 43 and 44].

Mr. White, like myself, had been burned out of house and home. He had removed with his family to a place of safety, and I had no idea where he or anyone else connected with the *Tribune* office might be found. My first point to make was naturally the site of our late office; but, before I reached it, I met two former tenants of our building, who told me that there was a job-printing office on Randolph Street, on the West Side, that could probably be bought. I immediately started for the West Side, and, while making my way through the crowd over the Madison Street bridge, desolation stared me in the face at every step, and yet I was much struck with the tone and temper of the people. On all sides I saw evidences of true Chicago spirit, and men said to one another, "Cheer up; we'll

be all right again before long," and many other plucky things. Their courage was wonderful. Everyone was bright, cheerful, pleasant, and even inclined to be jolly, in spite of the misery and destitution which surrounded them, and which they shared. One and all said, "Chicago must and shall be rebuilt at once."

On reaching Canal Street, on my way to purchase the printing-office I had heard of, I was informed that while Mr. White and I were saving our families, on Monday afternoon, Mr. Medill, seeing that the *Tribune* office must inevitably be burned, had sought for and purchased Edward's job-printing office, No. 15 Canal Street, where he was then busy organizing things. When I arrived there I found Mr. Medill in the upper stories among the types and printers, doing all he could to get ready to issue a paper in the morning. I saw at a glance that my work was below. The basement and main floor were filled with boards and boxes and rubbish, and these must be cleaned out at once. I placed a gang of men, under the command of our cashier, to clear out the main floor, and another gang, under a boss, to clear out the basement to receive a load of paper. I then went foraging for brooms, but the market was bare of the article, and I borrowed some of a neighbor.

Seeing that business was going on lively, my next duty was to get up four stoves. For these I started west on Randolph Street, but every store had sold out, till I got to the corner of Halsted Street. I found here the four I wanted—price, $16 each; told the owner I wanted all his men to go to work at once to get the pipe ready; but fearing if he did not know who had bought them, somebody with cash in hand might "jump my claim," I told him they were for the *Tribune* Company; that we had plenty of money in our vault and in the bank, and as soon as we could get at it he should have his pay. "I don't know about dat," said the worthy Teuton; "I guess I must have de money for dem stoves."

The thing amused me at the rapid change the fire had wrought. On Saturday our note would have been good for $100,000, and on Tuesday we could not buy four stoves and the fixtures on credit. In the best of humor, I told him to come with me and measure the height of the holes for pipe in the chimneys, and before he could get the articles ready he should have his money. This he did; and then my first question, half joke, half earnest, to every friend I met was, "Have you got any money?" The tenth man, perhaps,

Plate 44. The wasteland that was a city, the ruins of Chicago as seen from Harrison Street between Wabash and Michigan Avenues. On the left, partially visible, is the First Presbyterian Church on Wabash Avenue; on the right is St. Paul's Universalist Church, on Wabash Avenue at Van Buren Street. Many prominent Chicagoans had homes in this area. (Courtesy of the Chicago Historical Society)

Honorable Edward Cowles, of Cleveland, Ohio, said, "Yes, how much do you want?" "All you can spare"; and he handed me $60. Not enough for the stove genius; but I walked rapidly to his den, shook the greenbacks at him, and told him to hurry up, for I'd soon have the balance; came back to our office and found a dozen or more of our leading citizens, all "strapped," like myself, till at last E. S. Wadsworth, Esq., handed me $100. Messrs. Cowles and Wadsworth, therefore, furnished the cash capital to start the *Tribune* the next day after the fire. But money soon began to flow in.

Between three and four o'clock, our clerk, Mr. Lowell, came to me and said, "There are some people here with advertisements for lost friends." I said, "Take them and the cash, registering in your memorandum book"; and upon a dirty old box on the window sill for a desk, the *Tribune* at once commenced doing a lively business. A gentleman called me by name and said, "I haven't a morsel of food for my wife and children tonight, and not a cent to buy any; may I paint *'Tribune'* over your door?" It was soon done—bill, $3.75. And thus a family was provided for that night at least, and another citizen started up in business.

By 4 P.M. the stoves were up; Mr. White was duly installed with the editors in the rear of the main floor; the clerks were taking advertisements; the paper was soon after going into the basement; arrangements were made to print on the *Journal* press, our next door neighbor. Mr. Medill had his printers all in order; and a council was called, a list of materials made out, and it was agreed that I should start for Buffalo and New York that evening to get them. I hurried home, got my satchel—alas, clean linen was not to be had—and back to the office.

About eight, I took the middle of Canal Street, and went south to Twelfth, thence east to Clark, and thence south to Sixteenth, and just saw the cars moving away. Nothing was to be done but to return to 607 Wabash Avenue. I have mentioned my route thus particularly, to add that this was one of the most lonely and fearful tramps of my life. No street lamps, few people in the streets, and there were good reasons to give them as wide a berth as possible.

Another sleepless night; and in the morning as I sat sipping my coffee over some cold ham, I saw Sheridan's boys, with knapsack and musket, march proudly by. *Never did deeper emotions of joy overcome me.* Thank God, those most dear to me, and the city as well, are safe; and I hurried away to the train. *Had it not been for General Sheridan's prompt, bold, and patriotic action,*[1] I verily believe what was left of the city would have been nearly, if not quite entirely, destroyed by the cutthroats and vagabonds who flocked here like vultures from every point of the compass [Plate 45].

[1] The "boys in blue," whom General Sheridan telegraphed for were companies of the 5th United States Infantry, then commanded by Colonel Nelson A. Miles—later Brigadier-General—and stationed at Fort Leavenworth. Immediately on receipt of the dispatch the companies were placed on the cars and rushed through to Chicago. Governor Bross was not the only citizen who, in that fearful time, thanked God when the solid mass of bluecoats and glittering muskets represented the barrier to the mob that these companies did—giving definite assurance of the might of the law in every gun and in every soldier.—*Andreas's History of Chicago.*

Lambert Tree

[Judge of the Circuit Court of Cook County from 1870 to 1875, Tree (Plate 46) was Minister to Belgium and later to Russia during the administration of Grover Cleveland. The manuscript of his account is in the possession of the Chicago Historical Society.]

My residence at the time of the fire was at No. 282 Ohio Street, on the south side of the street, between Cass and State streets. The members of my household consisted, at the time, of my wife, my son Arthur, then eight years of age, my father, a man seventy years old, and my sister Ellen, and servants. We retired at about ten o'clock Sunday evening. At twelve o'clock I was awakened by my wife, who told me that a large fire seemed to be raging in the South Division, and, on going to a window in the rear of the house, I found a very serious conflagration was in progress in the direction of my office, which was at the corner of La Salle and Randolph streets. I hastily dressed and hurried across the river.

When I arrived at the building where my office was located, the roof and cupola of the Courthouse were already beginning to burn; several other buildings south and west of the Courthouse were in flames, and the air was full of sparks, cinders, and pieces of flaming felt torn from the roofs of the houses, and being carried in a northeasterly direction by the wind, whch was blowing a gale.

I went upstairs to my office, which was so light from the burning buildings in the neighborhood that I found it unnecessary to turn on the gas. Unlocking the safe, I took out as many papers and other things that I deemed valuable as I could stow in the pockets of my overcoat and a small tin box, and then, locking it again, I started for home.

My route on my return was down Randolph to Clark, up that street to Lake, along Lake to State, across State Street bridge, and thence on North State until I reached Ohio Street. When I got out of doors I found it literally raining fire. Along Randolph and Clark streets canvas awnings in front of many of the stores, and in several instances the large wooden signs, also, were burning. Here and there where the sparks had found a lodgment small jets of flames were darting out from wooden cornices on the tops of buildings, while the sparks and cinders which were constantly falling upon the streets were being whirled

Plate 46. *An engraving of Lambert Tree, who was Judge of the Circuit Court of Cook County from 1870 to 1875 and later United States Minister to Belgium and Russia. (Courtesy of the Chicago Historical Society)*

around in little eddies and scattered down the basement stairways.

As I crossed State Street bridge, I observed an occasional plank burning in the wooden footways of the bridge. Along North State and Ohio streets, the dead leaves which the wind had from time to time caught up and deposited against and under the wooden sidewalks had been ignited in many places by the flying sparks, which had in turn set fire to the sidewalks, so that every few yards tongues of fire were starting up between the cracks in the boards. Up to time of reaching home, however, I could not discover that any house was on fire on the North Side.

As soon as I reached my home I directed everybody to dress, and prepare to leave if necessary. I then went to the rear of the house, and on looking out of the window, observed that the railroad depot and Wright's livery stable, near the north end of State Street bridge, were burning. When I passed there less than ten minutes afterward, the little wooden cottage on the west of me was in flames. This cottage was four blocks north of Wright's livery stable, and, as far as I could discover, there were no buildings intervening between these two points which had yet taken fire; but it was one of the characteristic features of the conflagration that isolated buildings would catch fire several blocks in advance of the main body of the flames from the flying sparks and cinders.

I went upon the roof of my house, and ordered the servants to pass me up buckets of water as fast as they could, thinking that if I wet the roof thoroughly that would at least be a safeguard. In a few moments, however, I became convinced that no amount of water that I could command would save us.

The sparks and flaming felt were now flying as thickly on the North Side as I had, a short time before, observed them in the South Division. The size of some of this burning material hurled through the air seems quite incredible. While on the roof of my house, a burning mass, which was fully as large as an ordinary bed-pillow, passed over my head. It fell upon the street, and on descending I had the curiosity to examine it, and found it to be a mass of matted hay. There were also pieces of burning felt, some of which I should say were fully a foot square, flying through the air, and dropping upon the roofs of houses and barns.

By this time (which was about half-past two o'clock in the morning), a great many affrighted men, women, and children began to appear in the streets, hurrying along, carrying large bundles in their arms and upon their backs, or dragging trunks and boxes. Many of the neighbors were depositing trunks, pictures, and other things which they could most readily remove, into the grounds of H. H. Magie, on the opposite side of the street, it being supposed that a space so remote from buildings must be safe.

Two of our servants, catching the general infection to flee, dragged their trunks downstairs, and disappeared in the street. It began to be apparent to the rest of us that we also must seek a safer place. The burning cottage on the west of us, which was now enveloped in flames, and one or two barns on our premises, which had just taken fire, admonished us that our turn would soon come. It was, therefore, determined that we should cross the street and join Mr. and Mrs. Magie at their house, where we could await the further progress of events.

It was now nearly three o'clock, I should think. The ladies put on their bonnets, and my wife, carrying a tin box containing her jewelry and some other valuables, led the way, accompanied by my little son Arthur, my father and sister, and a faithful French girl, who remained with us through our subsequent adventures that night, and, by her coolness and nerve, proved most serviceable. I remained behind a few minutes to secure a trunk containing the family silver, and, as I dragged it through the hall, I also thought I would save a portrait of my son, which was hanging in the parlor. Accordingly I stepped in, cut the cords by which it was suspended, and carried it in one hand, while I drew the trunk across the street with the other. When halfway across the street, I turned and saw that we had left the house with a full head of gas turned on in all the rooms. It was hard to realize that we had left it for the last time.

When I reached Mr. Magie's garden, following the example of neighbors, I deposited my picture under a large tree, and it was the last I ever saw of it. The trunk containing the silver met a better fate. Not knowing exactly what to do with it, I delivered it to Mr. Magie's gardener, old Matthew, whom I happened to run across, with directions to bury it. He obeyed my instructions, as I found out the next morning; and this was the only property saved by the whole family.

I entered Mr. Magie's house by the back door; and as I was approaching it I saw that his stable, which was back on Ontario Street, was in flames. I found the family all assembled in the library, together with the mother of Mrs. Sylvester S. Bliss, one of our neighbors, who having become in some way separated from her own family, had, like ourselves, taken refuge in Mr. Magie's house. We had been there only a few moments, when, on looking out of the window I discovered that the covered wooden porch which was stretched across the whole width of Mr. Magie's house was on fire, and urged that we should immediately depart, as it was dangerous to remain a moment longer. All agreed to this, and we started to leave—my wife, my son, and myself leading the way.

We had scarcely got out of the door before we were assailed by a hurricane of smoke, sparks, and cinders, which nearly blinded and suffocated us. Fearing separation, I grasped my wife by one hand and my son by the other, and moved around to the west side of the house, intending to pass through one of the gates on Ohio Street; but we had no sooner got from under the protection which the north wall of the house afforded us, than we met the full force of this hurricane of smoke and fire. My wife's and sister's bonnets and my father's and son's hats were immediately blown from their heads, while the cinders were falling upon heads, hands, and faces, and burning them. It was impossible to get to the gate on Ohio Street before being suffocated, and we instinctively turned and ran towards the northeast corner of the block, thus turning our backs to the smoke.

I now observed that the paling fence, six feet high, which surrounded the block, as well as the wooden

Plate 47. Devastation near the Waterworks on Pine Street, now North Michigan Avenue. The Water Tower, left, was one of the few structures to survive the fire. (Courtesy of the Chicago Historical Society)

sidewalks on the outside of it, were on fire in many places, and that a great number of bushes, shrubs, and plants, and several of the trees in the grounds were burning. As we moved along, to add to the embarrassment of the situation, my wife and sister both showed signs of fainting, and the French girl now had the other arm of my wife, assisting her along.

Here I must record a circumstance which seemed almost providential at the time. There was no gate at the northeast corner of the block. We were simply driven in that direction by the storm of fire and smoke, because we could go in no other, I was, therefore, feeling very anxious about what we should be able to do after arriving at the fence, when, as we got within a few steps of it, about twenty feet of the fence fell over upon the sidewalk, and made a passageway for us. This was undoubtedly caused by the posts having been burned away in part near the ground, and the fury of the storm against the fence with its weakened supports. The fence fell upon the sidewalk, which was in full blaze, and thus we passed over it. The skirt of my wife's dress took fire as we went through the flames, and I tore it off.

When we had reached the street and counted our party we found to our horror, that neither Mr. nor Mrs. Magie were with us. It seemed, as we afterward learned, that instead of following us, as we had supposed when we all started from the house, they lingered behind for a few moments, and thus got separated from us. It was as impossible to go back then as it would have been to have crossed a sea of fire, and there was nothing to do but to continue our flight.

Our party, as we stood at the corner of Cass and Ontario streets, consisted of those I have mentioned already as having left my house to go to Mr. Magie's, with the addition of the mother of Mrs. Bliss. I also discovered, when we reached the street, that my wife, in her fright, had thrown away, in the grounds, the box which contained her jewelry and other valuables. It was too late to go back for it. My wife, sister, son, and the mother of Mrs. Bliss were all slightly burned about their heads, hands, and faces, and the clothes of all of us had numerous holes burned in them. My wife, sister, and son were also hatless. Beyond this we were all right; and we hastened eastward along Ontario Street, doubly oppressed by the feeling of uncertainty which now weighed upon us all as to the fate of Mr. and Mrs. Magie. Looking behind me, everything was enveloped in clouds of smoke and sparks, and here and there a neighbor's house was in flames.

OVER: *Plate 48. The fearful vision of a great city in flames. The white ribbon in the center of the picture is the Chicago River. (Harper's Weekly, October 28, 1871)*

We continued along Ontario Street until we struck the vacant grounds on the shore of the lake. These grounds then occupied a space from St. Clair Street to the lake, and from Superior to about Indiana or Illinois Street, covering many acres—perhaps forty or fifty.

On the north were Lill's brewery and the Waterworks [Plate 47], running to the water's edge, and preventing any advance beyond Superior Street in that direction, especially as both of these buildings were then on fire; on the south were one or two planing-mills and numerous lumberyards extending to the river. When we arrived on the lake shore we found thousands of men, women, and children, and hundreds of horses and dogs, who had already fled there for refuge. The grounds were dotted all over at short intervals with piles of trunks, chairs, tables, beds, and household furniture of every description. It seemed as if this great open space, with nothing but the broad lake on the east of us, ought to be safe; and yet there, a few hours later, and for the second time that morning, we nearly perished from suffocation.

It was between three and four o'clock when we arrived on the grounds. We stood among the crowd, watching the fire as it advanced and gradually encircled us, until the whole city in every direction, looking north, west, and south, was a mass of smoke and flames [Plate 48]. The crowd itself was a study. In some instances whole families were huddled around their little piles of furniture, which was all they had left that morning of their yesterday's home. Here and there a mother sat upon the ground clinging to her infant, with one or more little ones, who, exhausted by the prolonged interruptions to their slumbers, were now sleeping, with their heads reclining on her lap, as peacefully as if nothing unusual was transpiring. Several invalids lay helplessly stretched upon mattresses, but still surrounded by relatives and friends, who were endeavoring to soothe their fears. One young girl sat near me, with a cage containing a canary bird in her lap, whose life she was seeking to protect. She had covered the cage with her shawl, and from time to time raised it to see if the bird was all right. An hour or two later, while she was moving to a place of greater safety, I saw her little pet tumble from its perch to the bottom of the cage. It was dead; and the poor child, who doubtless had met her first sorrow, burst into tears.

There was also something of that demoralization visible which, it is said, so often crops out when the good ship has struck upon a lee shore and total shipwreck is inevitable. Some men and women who had found liquor among the household stores there, and who sought to drown their present woes in the bottle, were now reeling about, drunk; while in several other instances rough-looking men were going around breaking open and rifling trunks and boxes.

Judges of courts and police officers were there, but they only formed so many units in that stricken assemblage, and their authority that morning was no greater than that of any other man upon the ground. A poor woman, extremely ill, who had been brought down on a mattress, died in the midst of a mixed crowd of men, women, and children; and, although the fact that she had died was understood in the vicinity of where she lay, it did not seem to excite the sensation of horror which one would ordinarily expect at the happening of an event like this, under such circumstances; on the contrary, a knowledge of the fact seemed to be received with comparative indifference. Yet so solemn an incident as the transition from life to death of a human being in the presence of the same people differently situated would doubtless have excited the profoundest sympathy and kindest attention to the friends who stood hovering around the body. That such an event could occur in the midst of such a class of persons and cause no greater attention than it did simply furnishes an illustration of the state of people's minds, and the immediate danger in which they believed themselves to be standing that morning.

The sparks and cinders were falling as fast and thick as hailstones in a storm; and soon after daylight, to our discomfort and danger, the piles of household stuff which covered the ground everywhere began to burn. Among this stuff were many feather beds and hair mattresses, and the heat and smoke became so intense that we were obliged, from time to time, to change our position to one nearer the water [Plate 49].

An hour later, and the immense piles of lumber on the south of us were all afire, and then came the period of our greatest trial. Dense clouds of smoke and cinders rolled over and enveloped us, and it seemed almost impossible to breathe. Man and beast alike rushed to the water's edge, and into the water, to avoid suffocation. There was a mixed mass of human beings, horses, dogs, truck-wagons, and vehicles of all descriptions there. Some persons drove their horses into the lake as far as the poor beasts could safely go, and men, women, and children waded out and clambered upon the wagons to which the horses were attached, while the lake was lined with people who were standing in the water at various depths, from their knees to their waists, all with their backs to the storm of fire which raged behind them.

We remained in this position several hours, until the lumberyards were substantially destroyed, and the intensity of the heat and smoke had, in some measure, subsided. I then moved slowly with my family north along the water's edge as far as the foot of Superior Street—which, indeed, was as far north as one could go on the lake shore, the burning ruins of Lill's brewery and dock making a bar to further progress in that direction.

Plate 49. *A fire engine was a rare sight during the holocaust. This one has been placed on a barge in the Chicago River. In the background a coal pile still smolders. (Photograph by Jex Bardwell, courtesy of the Chicago Historical Society)*

At the foot of Superior Street there was a wooden one-story which had been erected for some manufacturing purpose, and which by some sort of miracle, had escaped the fire; and as we were all suffering intensely with our eyes, in consequence of the heat and smoke to which they had been subjected, we determined to enter the place. We found it already very much crowded with people, and, after trying it for a short time, concluded that the open air, even with the heat and smoke, could be no worse; and therefore came out and sought a position behind the north wall of Superior Street, which had been extended quite to the lake shore. My wife, being very much fatigued, took a seat on the ground, but had been there only a few moments when I discovered that her clothes were on fire. I immediately raised her, and succeeded in extinguishing the fire with my hands. We became satisfied that the safest place was on our feet, moving around, and waiting patiently until relief should come.

Between five and six o'clock in the afternoon I discovered a vehicle emerging from the smoke which still enveloped the city, although all the houses in this portion of it had already been destroyed. It was coming down Superior Street toward the lake, and I ran for-ward to meet it. It proved to be a covered one-horse grocery wagon; and I soon bargained with its driver to take as many as we could get into it, to the West Side, for ten dollars. Accordingly, my wife, son, father, sister, the mother of Mrs. Bliss, the French girl, and myself, and also Mr. and Mrs. Butterfield, their daughter Clara, and their son Justin, with his pet goat, which he had been carefully trying to shelter and protect through the day, all packed ourselves into the wagon and started for the West Side. The smoke was still so dense that we could see but little, and really had to grope our way along; but we saw enough to know that the North Side at least was destroyed [Plates 50 and 51], and that all that was left of the thousands of happy homes of the day before were a few chimney stacks and an occasional broken and cracked wall. All the rest lay in the smoldering embers and tangled debris of the cellars. Our course was taken along Superior Street to Clark, down Clark to Kinzie, and across Kinzie Street bridge, which fortunately escaped the fire, to the West Side.

When we arrived on the west side of the river, the driver asked me where we wanted to go. That question puzzled us all. We did not know,—anywhere, so that we could get a night's shelter and something to eat. It was now seven o'clock, and the last time that any of my family had partaken of food was at our five o'clock dinner on the preceding evening, twenty-six hours before. The man drove us up Washington Street, and stopped in front of a house, which he said was a boardinghouse. While descending from the wagon I was recognized by Mr. Charles Gray, who kindly invited my family, all he could accommodate, to come to his house, which was in the immediate vicinity, and where we were most hospitably treated by him and his wife, and everything they could think of to make us comfortable was done for us. Mr. and Mrs. Butterfield and the rest found quarters at the boardinghouse.

That night was an extremely anxious one to all of us. Everyone felt nervous lest some change of wind might cause another conflagration on the West Side; and as the supply of water was now entirely cut off, it could not be otherwise than disastrous. The streets were patrolled by citizens, who had organized them into districts for the purpose; and I, although somewhat fatigued, walked the district in which we were staying the greater part of the night. So timid did everyone feel about fire, that smoking was prohibited on the streets; and it was one of the duties of the patrol to see that this regulation was carried out. An idea seemed also to prevail in the public mind that we stood in peril of incendiarism. I did not remove my clothes during the night.

At daybreak, I hailed an express wagon, and drove over to the North Side, to see if I could find the trunk of silver which I had directed to be buried. When we

Plate 50. *Dearborn and Ohio Streets, in the heart of the fashionable residential section of the North Side, after the fire. (Courtesy of the Chicago Historical Society)*

reached the North Side, everything was the picture of desolation. Not a house remained to the north, south, or east of Wells Street as far as the eye could reach, save only that of Mahlon D. Ogden. The telegraph wires lay curled and tangled upon the streets, and here and there was a dead horse, cow, or animal of some kind, which had been overtaken by the fire, and perished. I saw that morning, however, but one dead human body, and that was on Dearborn between Ohio and Ontario streets. It was burned beyond recognition.

When I reached Mr. Magie's grounds, I found that old Matthew had faithfully executed my orders, and that the trunk and its contents were safe; and this was

the only piece of personal property which remained to us after the fire. I put it into the express wagon, and drove back to Mr. Gray's house, where we all sat down to an excellent breakfast.

I will now return to Mr. and Mrs. Magie. Their story, as related by themselves, is that instead of following us out of the house, as we supposed at the time, they remained a few moments to gather up a few keepsakes. That when they did come out, they encountered the same tornado which we had experienced, and were also driven back in their at-

Plate 51. *St. James Protestant Episcopal Church, a North Side landmark at the southeast corner of Cass and Huron Streets, whose parishioners included some of Chicago's oldest families. The church tower and part of the facade were restored and appear today much as they did before the fire. (Courtesy of the Chicago Historical Society)*

tempt to pass out of the gates on Ohio Street. They then, instead of going to the northeast corner of the block, as we had done, went to the northwest corner of it, where an immense elm tree stood, and which they thought would give them some shelter from the sparks and cinders which were falling upon and burning them terribly. After they had remained in this position for a short time, and when they supposed they were lost, they discovered a hole burned in the bottom of the fence on the State Street side, three or four feet long and two or three feet high, through which they crawled, and thus escaped into the street. They were by this time, however, badly burned upon their ears, noses, hands, and limbs. They made their way up State Street to Chicago Avenue, along that street to La Salle, and up the last street some distance, when a friendly door was thrown open to them. They had only been there a few hours, however, when the house in which they had taken refuge was threatened with destruction by the advancing fire, and they were obliged again to seek a place of safety.

Following the crowd of fugitives northward as rapidly as their blistered limbs would permit, they reached North Avenue, along which they walked until they found themselves, late in the afternoon, on the western outskirts of the city, completely exhausted by fatigue and suffering. (It should be stated that Mr. and Mrs. Magie were both approaching seventy years of age at the time.) While standing upon the road, not knowing what to do, they were met by Dr. Gillett, a gentleman who had known Mr. Magie in former years and now recognized him. He kindly procured an express wagon, the only conveyance which was to be had, and assisting Mr. and Mrs. Magie into it, drove them immediately to his own house; so that, in addition to a comfortable shelter that night, the burns of Mr. and Mrs. Magie, which had now become most painful, received immediate and skillful medical attention from Dr. Gillett.

Such was the total disorganization of the city immediately after the fire, that it was only after three days of the most diligent search that we were able to learn whether Mr. and Mrs. Magie were still alive, and of their whereabouts. On finding them, we were all united under the hospitable roof of Mr. Stanford, where we remained a few days and until we could find a house to rent, which was no easy matter at that time.

[The Haines H. Magie property was part of the Kinzie addition to Chicago, and remained in the original ownership of the Magie family, never being subdivided, but passing into the hands of Judge Tree through his wife, who was Miss Anna Magie. The brown stone Tree mansion stood there until the death of Judge Tree, and the site is now (1915) marked by the Medinah Temple and the Tree Studio Building. ED.]

Arthur M. Kinzie

[Kinzie was a grandson of John Kinzie, the first permanent white settler of Chicago. The manuscript of his account is in the possession of the Chicago Historical Society.]

I had been, for the last two years previous to October, 1871, at the North Manitou Island, near the lower end of Lake Michigan. Having decided to return to Chicago, I arrived here with my family and household goods on Friday, October 6th, and took up quarters temporarily at the residence of my uncle, Colonel Robert A. Kinzie, on Ontario Street, nearly opposite the Historical Society's building, between Clark and Dearborn streets [Plates 52 and 53]. All of our furniture and effects were placed in a storage warehouse, corner of Cass and Michigan streets, I having refused an offer to store them on the West Side because the building was of wood, and I was afraid they might be burned before we got settled in a house of our own.

On Sunday evening I had been on the South Side visiting my brother, and was returning home between eight and nine o'clock, when the fire alarm was sounded. After I had reached home and saw how rapidly the fire was increasing, I left the house and went toward the fire. I sat at the south entrance of the La Salle Street tunnel for some time, until the buildings southwest of the Courthouse Square took fire, and then started home, convinced that the fire would sweep all the way to the Illinois Central Depot, but not for an instant believing it would cross the river. I remember thinking how scared a woman must be who, at the north entrance of the tunnel, asked me if I thought the fire would reach there.

On arriving at Colonel Kinzie's, I found that he had just returned, having been over to his office at the United States Army headquarters to secure some valuable vouchers, which he barely succeeded in accomplishing, and that our wives had gone to look at the fire. I retired to my room, and sat reading for some time, when, on looking out of the window toward the south, I saw that the fire was on the North Side. My wife had not returned, so I aroused my two children, and commenced to dress them. At this time the policemen on duty were going from house to house rapping on the doors and telling the people not to go to bed, but to be ready to move on short notice. In a short time my wife and aunt returned, and stated that

they had been trying to stamp out the fire in the leaves around Magie's place.

At this juncture, Mrs. Captain Johnson came running in, wild with excitement, and asking us all if our clothes were insured, rushed away again. Just then a boy pounded on the door, rang the bell furiously, and shouted, "Mr. Kinzie your house is on fire!" Hastily running upstairs to the back of the house, I found it to be a fact, and seizing a blanket from the bed, I took one of the children, my wife taking the other, and we left the house—to go, we knew not where. Turning north on Dearborn Avenue, we walked slowly along, scarcely realizing that we were not to return shortly, as if nothing had happened of a serious nature.

When we arrived opposite Mr. Mahlon D. Odgen's house, my wife suggested going in there until the fire was over; but as I could not see how that was any safer place than where we had left, I decided to move on. A short distance farther on my wife declared she must stop and rest and get a drink of water, so we went into Obadiah Jackson's house, which we were passing at that time. Mrs. Jackson was very kind, but there was no water to be obtained, the Waterworks having ceased operating. She had, however, some very nice bottled ale which she gave us; and as we were enjoying that and resting, the gas suddenly went out and we were left in darkness. Mr. Jackson's carriage was at the door, and Mrs. Jackson was busy packing the silver, and such articles as they could carry with them, intending to depart as soon as the near approach of the fire forced them to do so.

After resting a while longer, we started on again. Every block or two we would sit down on the edge of the sidewalk, and rest until the fire made us move onward. Very little was said by anyone; there was no loud talking or shouting, though the streets were crowded with people and vehicles of every description, loaded with every conceivable kind of luggage. I saw one man carrying the rubber tube and broken standard of a droplight; another was trundling a wheelbarrow on which was a cookstove, while on his back was a huge featherbed. One woman had a live hen in her arms, several had cats, and numbers had canary

Plate 52. This house, built for Colonel Robert A. Kinzie at the northwest corner of Rush and Michigan (later Hubbard) Street, was one of the many grand residences that burned on Chicago's North Side. Colonel Kinzie, a son of the Chicago pioneer, John Kinzie, was not living in the house at the time of the Fire. The formally attired figures are most likely friends and relatives of Dr. Sidney Sawyer, who was living there when this photograph was taken in the 1860s. (Courtesy of the Chicago Historical Society)

birds in cages. We met Dr. Tolman Wheeler pulling a trunk along the sidewalk by one of the straps; and as he was going directly toward the fire instead of away from it, I turned him around and started him in the right direction.

Just after daylight, we reached the corner of Clark Street and North Avenue. At that place we found Hon. John Wentworth, accompanied by a boy carrying his black leather bag, whom he informed us was a bellboy from the Tremont House that he had impressed into his services when he left the hotel. We consulted as to the best route to take. He advocated going west across the river, as by so doing we would get out of the track of the flames and eventually arrive at a place of safety. My idea was to push on to Lake View, where we had friends, and trust to the fire burning itself out before it got that far. And so we parted, each taking the route we had decided upon.

At this time the whole appearance of things was most unnatural and solemn. The crowded streets and sidewalks; the incongruous heaps of humanity; the dust and smoke driven by the fierce gale which, with increasing force, was sweeping from the southwest; the lurid glare from the flames; and the silence which everyone maintained as they trudged wearily along, not knowing where they were going, nor where their enforced journey would end; together with the ever-falling sparks from the unrelenting and resistless wall of fire behind us, continually impelling us forward, all tended to make the scene one never to be forgotten, but impossible to fully describe.

A short time after leaving Mr. Wentworth and his bag-bearer, we took possession of an empty omnibus;

Plate 53. The ruins of the library building of the Chicago Historical Society, which stood on the north side of Ontario Street between Clark and Dearborn Streets. Arthur Kinzie was living in a house opposite the Historical Society at the time of the fire. (Courtesy of the Chicago Historical Society)

and leaving my wife and children therein, I repaired to a livery stable near at hand, to see if I could make a bargain for some sort of a conveyance to move us more comfortably from the immediate vicinity of the fire. The proprietor did not give up the hope that somehow or other his property would be spared, so he would not let anything go out until he had to move altogether. If I was a mind to wait, he said, until the fire made him travel, he would give me a lift. No offers of any price could move him from that decision. I heard afterward that he waited so long that he lost most of his stock.

When I returned to the omnibus, I found Mr. Thomas L. Forrest talking to my wife, and he kindly invited us to his house, a square or two distant, to rest and have some breakfast. This we gladly consented to do. Mr. Forrest and myself went up on the roof of his home. The sight was truly awful! Towards the south nothing to be seen but what seemed a solid wave of smoke and fire rolling slowly towards us, the latter darting and leaping upward, it seemed, hundreds of feet. The wind was so strong that we could not stand on the roof without holding on to something. When we were moving along Wells Street I could see, as I looked back occasionally, the fire make a jump across the street from west to east and strike a building; the front would melt away, exactly as a sheet of paper laid on a bed of burning coals will smoulder while, then suddenly flash up and be gone. I also observed burning pieces of boards sailing along, high over our heads, that were certainly six feet long and as many inches wide.

When it became evident later in the day that our kind host's refuge would soon become untenantable, we resumed our enforced pilgrimage. Before we left there I was out on the street when I was accosted by Ira Bowen, seated in a one-horse wagon loaded with his Lares and Penates, who said, with the tears making light-colored streaks down his dusky cheeks, "Arth., have you seen my wife and baby? I've lost them!" I answered, "No," and inquired where he had lost them. He said that he had got into his store wagon, put his wife and baby into his carriage, and told the driver to follow him, but, on looking around a short while before, they were nowhere to be seen. He said, "My store is burned; my house is burned; everything is burned; but I won't care for it all, if I can only find my wife and baby." I asked him where he was intending to go when he started, and he said he thought of going to Mrs. Reynolds'. He said he

had not been there yet, so I suggested that he do so;
and he found them there.

The rest of the trip to the city limits was much the
same as the first part of the journey. We saw thousands encamped in Lincoln Park, each group surrounded by the few household effects they had been
able to save and transport to that place. On arriving
at the city limits, we found Colonel Robert Kinzie's
family comfortably settled at the hospitable mansion
of Robert Clarke, who, with his family, were busily
engaged cooking and distributing food to the famish-
ing refugees who crowded the grounds and adjacent
street.

After remaining a short time we accepted the in-
vitation of John Hunter, the conductor of the Lake
View dummy, to make his house at Graceland our
home, and reached there about dark on Monday. The
neighboring woods contained a goodly number of
outcasts, and the streetcars, which had been run up
there for safety, made a comfortable shelter for many.
A number of the inhabitants of that vicinity were at
work with plows and spades, digging trenches and
ditches to prevent the fire from passing through
Wright's Woods.

During the evening the prairie to the west of us
took fire, and we began to think that, after all, the
lake would be the only sure refuge from the devouring
element. That fire, however, shortly burned itself out,
which relieved our minds very much. About midnight
I heard someone call my name, and running out, I
found, with what gratitude to God no one can tell, a
carriage containing my brother George and my
brother-in-law, who had started at noon, on Monday,
from Indiana Avenue near Twelfth Street, and by
driving around on the West Side, and thence to the
North Side, had succeeded in getting in front of the
fire and tracking us to that place. The carriage was
loaded with provisions and jugs of water. I hastily
gathered my family, and bidding adieu to our kind
entertainers, we started for my wife's sister's, on the
South Side.

In passing through the vacant parts of the
Northwest Side, we distributed our provisions and
water to those we could find of the sick, who were encamped in large numbers in that vicinity. We saw in
one place a very sick man. His wife was attending
him, and had obtained an old piano packing case,
which she had placed on its side with the bottom
toward the wind, and made a bed for her husband in-
side. A piece of candle fastened to a wire hung from
the top, by the light of which she was reading to him.
Her greatest trouble was want of water, and when we
gave her a jugful her gratitude knew no bounds.

It was a strange sight as we passed through the
burned district that night. All the squares formerly
built up solidly were now so many black excavations,
while the streets had the appearance of raised turn-
pikes intersecting each other on a level prairie. All the
coalyards were still burning, and gave light enough to
travel without difficulty [Plate 54]. About daylight on
Tuesday we reached our destination, truly thankful
that we had escaped with our lives, and were provided
with shelter and kind friends while so many were
without either at that terrible time.

Mary L. Fales

[From a letter written by Mrs. David Fales to her mother, October 10, 1871, and now in the possession of the Chicago Historical Society.]

You have probably heard of our fire, and will be glad to know we are safe, after much tribulation. Sunday night a fire broke out on the West Side, about three miles southwest of us. The wind was very high, and David said it was a bad night for a fire. About two o'clock we were awakened by a very bright light, and a great noise of carts and wagons [Plate 55]. Upon examination, David found that the fire was not at all on the North Side, but was burning so furiously on the South Side that the whole sky was bright. They thought it would stop when it came to the river, but it proved no obstacle, and the North Side was soon on fire, and Wells and La Salle streets were crowded with carts and people going north.

We saw that with such a wind it would soon reach our neighborhood, and David told me to pack what I most valued. It seemed useless to pack in trunks, as every vehicle demanded an enormous price and was engaged. Several livery stables were already burned, and loose horses were plenty. One of the Wheeler boys had a horse given him for nothing, excepting a promise to lead it to a safe place. He took it home and tied it in their yard. Having no wagon, it was of no use to him, so David took it, and after a while succeeded in finding a no-top buggy; we felt very lucky, as nobody around could get either horse or conveyance. David packed it full, set me and himself on top, and started off to the Hutchinson's.

I cannot convey to you how the streets looked. Everybody was out of their houses, without exception, and the sidewalks were covered with furniture and bundles of every description. The middle of the street was a jam of carts, carriages, wheelbarrows, and every sort of vehicle—many horses being led along, all excited and prancing, some running away. I scarcely dared look right or left, as I kept my seat by holding tightly to the trunk. The horse would not be restrained, and I had to use all my powers to keep on. I was glad to go fast, for the fire behind us raged, and the whole earth, or all we saw of it, was a lurid yellowish red.

David left me at Aunt Eng's and went for another load of things. This he soon brought back, and he went off again, and I saw him no more for seven hours. People came crowding to Aunt Eng's, and the house was full of strangers and their luggage. One young lady, who was to have had a fine wedding tomorrow, came dragging along some of her wedding presents. One lady came with four servants, and one with six blankets of clothing. One lady came with nurse and baby, and, missing her little boy, went off to look for him; this was about daylight, and she did not come back at all. Now and then somebody's husband would come back for a minute; but there was work for everybody, and they only stayed long enough to say how far the fire advanced, and assured us of safety.

At twelve David came and said that he had taken everything out of our house, and buried the piano and

Plate 55. *A wagon loaded with household goods races through the streets, struggling to keep ahead of the flames. (Drawing by Alfred R. Waud, courtesy of the Chicago Historical Society)*

ABOVE: *Plate 56.* Ezra B. McCagg's residence, with its impressive conservatories, was a good example of the North Side mansions destroyed by the fire. The house stood on Clark Street facing Washington Square. (Courtesy of the Chicago Historical Society) BELOW: *Plate 57.* The New England Congregational Church at the corner of Dearborn Street and Delaware Place also faced Washington Square. It was a favorite house of worship in Chicago for transplanted Yankees. (Courtesy of the Chicago Historical Society)

The homeless taking refuge in a church

Plate 58. *"The Homeless Take Refuge in a Church."* (*Drawing by Alfred R. Waud, courtesy of the Chicago Historical Society*)

books, together with the china, in Mr. Hubbard's grounds. He saw persons taking off all the chairs, tables, and light furniture, without saying a word, for he knew they would burn, even in the street, and my nice preserves, which Maggie had set out on the piazza, he gave freely to anybody who cared to take them.

The Hubbards thought they were safe in a brick house with so much ground around it; but wet their carpets and hung them over the wooden facings for additional safety. It was all to no purpose. David saw ours burn and fall; then theirs shared the same fate. The McCagg's large house and stables burned in a few minutes, also the New England Church and Mr. Collyer's [Plates 56 and 57]. In the afternoon the wind blew more furiously, the dust was blinding, the sky gray and leaden, and the atmosphere dense with smoke. We watched the swarms of wagons and people pass. All the men, and many of the women, were dragging trunks by cords tied in the handles; the

children were carrying and pulling big bundles.

Soon they saw Aunt Eng's house must go too. Then such confusion as there was! Everybody trying to get a cart, and not one to be had at any price. After a while, two of the gentlemen who had wagons carried their wives farther north, and those that were left watched for empty wagons, but nobody spoke a word. Mr. Hutchinson, David, and some others, were taking things out and burying them, and many of the ladies fairly lost their wits. Poor Aunt Eng even talked of sending home a shawl that somebody left there long ago. David started for a cart. Again he was successful, and got an old sand cart, with no springs, one board out of the bottom, with a horse that had not been out of harness for twenty-four hours. He put in all our things, and one trunk of Aunt Eng's, to which Miss M. added a bandbox.

The West Side was safe; but to get there was the question. The bridges were blocked and some burned, but the man who owned the cart thought we could get there. We thought of Judge Porter's and Mr. Dupee's, where we believed we would be welcome. Wherever Aunt Eng's family went, they must walk, and our prospects seemed so fair that we took May with us. Our ride was an anxious one. The horse had

Plate 59. *As soon as the embers of the fire had cooled, banks and jewelry stores began digging frantically to recover their safes and to open their vaults. (The* Illustrated London News, *November 11, 1871)*

been overused, and when urged on would kick till the old cart bid fair to break in pieces; then he would go on, and, finally, finding kicking no use, gave it up, much to my relief. Many times we were blocked, and it seemed as if the fire must reach the bridge before we did. But we were much too well off to complain.

Some carts had broken down, horses had given out, and many people were walking and pulling big things, and seemed almost exhausted. Furniture and clothing lay all along the road. Mrs. Hamilton hailed us from a mean little hut, two miles from her house and ours, and asked us to take a bag of Mr. Hubbard's silver. It must have been some servant's house. Anyway, it burnt soon after, and we still have the silver. The fences were broken in all the unbuilt fields; and furniture and people covered every yard of space. After a ride of two hours and a half we reached Judge Porter's at dusk, and found a warm welcome.

Every family I know on the North Side is burned

out. I can't enumerate them. It would be useless. It is sufficient to say every individual one. We were the only ones who took our things from Aunt Eng's. The lady with the six bundles left five behind her; the lady with the four servants left a bundle of French dresses to burn, but, worst of all, the baby and nurse. They went with the Hutchinsons. At the last minute, a Miss M. insisted on David taking charge of her watch; she said she could trust it to no one else, and it did not occur to her to keep it herself. All of our clothing is saved, and much we have with us.

I never felt so grateful in my life as to hear the rain pour down at three o'clock this morning. That stopped the fire.

The gentlemen have come in, and David says the piano burned under the ground; nothing was left but the iron plates. The North Side is level, as is the burned part of the South Side, so that the streets are not distinguishable. They say people in every class of life are out of doors. The churches are full, and food is sent to them, but hardly anyone has any to spare [Plate 58]. My watch was at the jeweler's, and may have been in a safe, but the safes have not yet been uncovered [Plate 59]. I shall write soon again; meanwhile, direct to 448 West Washington Street.

William A. Croffut

[At the time of the fire Croffut was managing editor of the *Chicago Evening Post*. His account is taken from the *Lakeside Monthly,* January, 1872.]

From that windy night when the first prophetic flame shot into the clouds and leaned like a crimson Pisa to the northeast till the last building fell and the destroyer had crept sullenly away into coal piles and garbage heaps there was a helpless acquiescence on the part of spectators that was pitiful. But when the raging fiend had died of plethora the old energy again came forth. Rigidity returned to the weakened spine, and vigor to the flaccid hand, and the eye of enterprise was lighted up once more with its undying flame. When the fire was baffled, citizens who had cowered and fled before it in awe arose bravely and said, "We can conquer everything else."

On every one of the hundred squares that had been laid in ashes on the South Side, men straightway attacked the smoking embers, extinguishing the lingering flames in order to build anew [Plate 60]. Pieces of iron, writhing in a thousand fantastic forms, and scarcely revealing under their strange disguises the original gas and water pipes, safes, scales, chandeliers, stoves, mantels, and columns they had been were pulled out while still warm, and carried away for foundry purposes. Ashes and broken bricks were carted to the lake and dumped to make more land for an already opulent railroad corporation. Walls were pulled down, and an army of men were employed to completely clear away the debris, and clean and square with a trowel such bricks as could be made available for rebuilding.

The first merchants who returned to the burnt district were, of course, the newsboys, peripatetic of habit and insinuating of demeanor. After the newspaper nomads came an apple-woman on Tuesday morning, who, with an air of mingled audacity and timidity, stationed her handcart at the corner of State and Randolph streets, half a mile within the ashen circle. She was the pioneer of all the trade of the future.

On Tuesday morning the last house burnt, away at the north. By Tuesday afternoon a load of new lumber had crept into the South Division [Plates 61 and 62]. On Wednesday morning that lumber was thrown into the form of a box to cover a merchant's wares. This was the inauguration of Slabtown [Plate 63]. Thenceforward there were innumerable cartings; heaps of charred rubbish were briskly exchanged for heaps of fresh pine; carpenters multiplied like locusts; the air assumed a resinous odor, and the clatter of hammers echoed as if the ruins were being knocked down to relic hunters by an enraged auctioneer.

By far the most grotesque phase of the calamity is the manner in which the vast business of the city, suddenly driven into the street, instantly accommodated itself to new locations and conditions. When the crimson canopy of Monday night merged into the dawn of Tuesday morning, it was found that, besides personal property, some thousands of loads of merchandise had been saved—stowed away in tunnels, buried in back alleys, piled up all along the lake shore, strewn in front yards through the avenues, run out of the city in boxcars, and even, in some instances, freighted upon the decks of schooners off the harbor. And, far more than this, five thousand merchants had saved their good name—that imperishable entity, that "incorporeal hereditament" which resists burglars and all the assaults of the elements, and carries an invisible treasury for him who wears its badge. Two hundred thousand people in the city, and ten times that number out of the city, were in immediate need of goods and compelled to buy [Plate 64].

It was at this juncture that the terrible descent of the barbarians upon our aristocratic thoroughfares began. Down Wabash and Michigan avenues, hitherto sacred to the "first families," rushed the Visigoths in a wild, irresistible horde, with speculation in their eyes. West Washington Street—prim and stately West Washington—was the next victim; then followed West Lake, Randolph, Madison, Monroe [Plate 65]. Block after block was swallowed up by the invaders. Trade walked into the houses with a yardstick for its stiletto, and domestic life took up its pack and retreated.

Many a man who has done a business of half a million a year has invaded his own front parlor on the avenue; has whisked the piano, the gorgeous sofas, the medallion carpet, and the clock of ormolu into the capacious upper stories, and has sent his family to keep them company; while showcases have been ar-

ABOVE: *Plate 60.* *Workmen clean up the debris shortly after the fire. (Photograph by Jex Bard-well, courtesy of the Chicago Historical Society)* BELOW: *Plate 61. Lumber and other supplies desperately needed by the destroyed city arrive at the mouth of the Chicago River. (Courtesy of the Chicago Historical Society)*

Plate 62. Fresh lumber is stacked in front of the gutted Michigan Central Railroad office on South Water Street. (Photograph by Jex Bardwell, courtesy of the Chicago Historical Society)

rayed through drawing and dining rooms, and clerks now serve customers with hats, furs, shoes, or jewelry, where they formerly spooned water ices at an evening party.

The burnt district looks as if Cheyenne had waltzed across the alkaline prairies and best-ridden our poor disreputable river; but the city for a mile west and south of the fine district looks like Vanity Fair. The carelessness, even recklessness, with which Commerce has dropped down into dwelling-houses, haphazard, is grotesque and whimsical to the last degree. Three or four kinds of business, moreover, are crowded under every roof. A shoe store is in the basement, with long strings of gaiters and slippers hanging where the hat rack was; a bench for customers improvised from an inverted box where the sideboard stood; fertile boxes of shoes are in the kitchen and coalhole. And over the front, five yards of outstretched cotton cloth bears the simple legend, "Shoes." Upstairs is a button factory, with pendulous and fascinating strings of buttons festooned across the aristocratic windows. The bedrooms higher up are lawyers', doctors', and insurers' offices; and into the dormer windows of the roof shoot a large quiver full of telegraphic wires.

The next building is a stylish structure with a bow front; a bank president occupied it in September, and is perchance still in exile in some of the upper stories—but the bow window in the parlor, scene of what countless sly flirtations and pleasant family siestas, is now garnished with ladies' stockings hung up in graduated array; while a brown balmoral swing, a silent sentinel, at the door, and the variety of feminine toggery here and there displayed complete the story of Mammon's invasion. Farther on is a pretty cream-colored cottage, the obvious creation of a pair who were at once lovers and artists. It is set a little distance from the walk; it has the angles and wings that are so charming and picturesque; a veranda runs cozily around it, and along and about it climbs a vine—a cool and delightful summer trellis. Here, too, the barbarians have effected an entrance and broken up the nest. Barrels of molasses and vinegar and flour lie impudently and lazily in the yard. A greasy-looking man goes into the door with a kerosene can, and a boy sidles out giving his undivided attention to candy. In the bay window is a symmetrical cob-house, constructed of bars of soap; and brooms, mops, and codfish are disclosed through the leafless trellis.

A little farther down the block a bevy of schoolgirls issue chattering from a ladies' fancy store; laces, collars, cuffs, velvet ribbon, and all the more delicate furniture of the female form are displayed in the window and revealed through the door ajar. A month ago this was a blacksmith shop, and the sparks flew

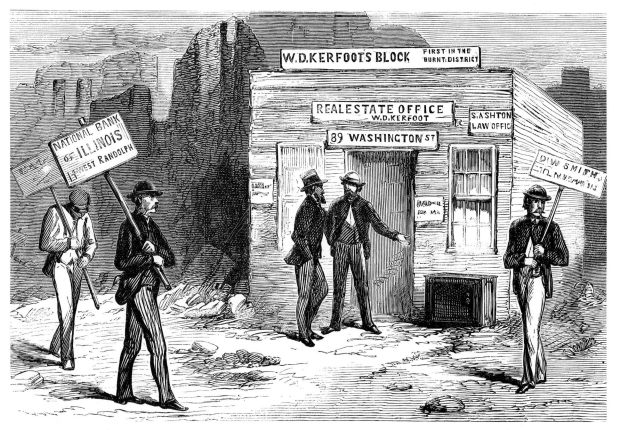

ABOVE: *Plate 63.* W. D. Kerfoot's real estate office on Washington Street, said to be the first business to reopen in the burned district. (Frank Leslie's Illustrated Newspaper, *November 11, 1871*) BELOW: *Plate 64.* One of the most serious problems faced by Chicagoans after the fire was the lack of shelter, for some 100,000 people were homeless. Wooden shanties, such as these on the North Side, were quickly thrown up in the cellars of burnt-out residences. (Harper's Weekly, *November 4, 1871*)

Plate 65. Temporary wooden buildings go up near the corner of Randolph and Market Streets. (Courtesy of the Chicago Historical Society)

in a fountain from the anvil, and the hammer clattered upon a horse's shoe. Scrubbing-brush and whitewash-brush have completely disguised the parvenu.

Down State Street to Twentieth, and here is the largest dry goods store in the city or the West—Field, Leiter & Co.'s. Here are hundreds of clerks and thousands of patrons a day, busy along the spacious aisles and the vast vistas of ribbons and laces and cloaks and dress-goods. This tells no story of a fire. The ladies jostle each other as impatiently as of old, and the boys run merrily to the incessant cry of "Cash." Yet, Madam, this immense bazaar was six weeks ago the horse barn of the South Side Railroad! After the fire, the hay was pitched out, the oats and harness and equine gear were hustled into another building, both

floors were varnished, and the beams were painted or whitewashed for their new service. Here where ready-made dresses hang then hung sets of double harness; yonder where a richly-robed body leans languidly across the counter and fingers point laces, a manger stood and offered hospitality to a disconsolate horse. A strange metamorphosis!—yet it is but an extreme illustration of the sudden changes the city has undergone.

All up and down Wabash and Michigan avenues on the South Side, and Monroe, Madison, Washington, Randolph, and Lake streets on the West Side, the fronts of the houses have been suddenly adapted to new uses; extensions have shot out from the basement to the sidewalk, resinous with the smell of new pine; and signs have appeared in all sorts of uncanny places—spiked to the handsome front door that servants in livery used to swing open upon its bronze hinges, sticking awkwardly from the oriole window where canaries used to sing, and even sprouting

WILLIAM A. CROFFUT 83

Plate 66. *Children were soon selling relics of the fire, for almost every Chicagoan and visitor wanted at least one piece of glass or iron which had been shaped into a grotesque form by the flames.* (Frank Leslie's Illustrated Newspaper, *November 11, 1871*)

strange arborescent growths from the bit of greensward between the sidewalk and the street, multicolored, huge, and cruciform, on duty like so many bucolic warnings to "look out for the locomotive." Ever since the fire, Chicago has been the Mecca of sign painters; and every man commanding a brush and paint pot was sure of constant employment at high wages, whether he could spell or not. Pine boards have become exhausted, and broad bands of white cotton have been introduced instead; and by such wrinkled insignia did some of the wealthiest of the national banks first indicate their retreat.

The churches that are spared have been curiously appropriated—several of them by the relief societies, others by institutions that are of the earth earthy. Here is one overrun and utterly deluged by Uncle Sam's mail—given up in all its parts to the exigencies of the city postal service. One is divided up for offices—a lawyer offers to defend your title; an insurance man volunteers to save you from the next fire; and in the recess that used to hold the choir, a dentist holds the heads and examines the mouths of his vic-

tims. Another church is turned into a watch factory; and still another is possessed by an express company, and over the official desks in the vestry-room vaults in a painted bow is the suggestive legend, "Come unto me, all ye that are heavy laden."

As already intimated, the work of rebuilding began the instant the fire withdrew. Indeed, for weeks before the flames were extinguished, while fierce volcanoes smoked and glowed in every block, and the vast heaps of anthracite threw forth angry pink and purple tongues, like the geysers of the Yellowstone, thousands of men were finding the old dimensions of the cellars and building up the stone foundations anew.

The burnt district in the South Division—the square mile bounded by the lake, river, and Harrison Street—is too valuable per front foot to furnish hospitality to sheds, barracks, and wooden warehouses like those that have found room elsewhere among the ashes. The real estate market. as far as there is a market, shows no great diminution below the prices asked and paid before the fire, and taxes over all these hundred blocks are still so heavy as to render prompt rebuilding imperative. So it happens that at the date of writing more than half the cellars again present the form of rectangular excavations swept and garnished for the builder's force.

On each side of every square, eager teams drag up the inclines into the street great loads of brick, stone,

Plate 67. *Within a month, Chicago was building a gleaming new city of brick and stone. This photograph shows Lake Street looking east from La Salle Street with the white stone Marine Building on the corner. (Courtesy of the Chicago Historical Society)*

iron, and ashes, and the foundation walls rise in their places again to the cheery cry of "Mort!" as, wooed by the strains of Amphion's lute, rose the conscious walls of Thebes.

In the cellars of warehouses, where great masses of iron were kept, in stove stores, scale stores, and wholesale stores of hoop-iron, men armed with drills, crowbars, huge sledgehammers, and blasting powder are toiling to disengage the mass. Even the iron was as straw in the furnace-blast of that awful morning—stoves, and sheet and pig iron all melted miserably and ran helplessly down, roaring with rage, to the ground, and there it cooled in all fantastic attitudes and shapes. Here is a hillock of solid iron, as large as an omnibus; there is a platform as large as Table Rock—it once was moulded into kitchen stoves; yonder are upright masses, some of them rearing like a centaur, and others writhing like the group of Laocoön; farther down the ruins is a building where the lower stratum of the flowing metal has cooled first, and subsequent cascades of iron have dashed over it and trickled through it like so much molasses; and beneath the drippings hang in iron crystal stalactites from an inch to six feet long, like the lime drippings of a cave! As these are the most marvelous of the relics, so they are the most difficult to dispose of, and the owners of the lots are now quarrying the ponderous masses with huge levers, blasting powder, and all the arts of engineering [Plate 66].

The walls of more than three hundred of the better class of brick and stone buildings are already rising in the South Division—rising even in midwinter, when masons are driven to cover in every other city north of 35°. Who thinks of using a trowel all through the winter months in New York, Boston, St. Louis, or even Cincinnati? Yet three thousand masons and bricklayers and mortar makers and carriers are regularly employed in Chicago all the week through as we write. Many builders have halted at the top of the cellar wall to wait for March, but hundreds of others are pushing vigorously upwards in spite of every obstacle presented by an extreme climate. It is December, but an artificial summer is created to keep the work from freezing up; a bonfire is blazing before the mortar bed, where the compound is prepared as the housewife prepares her dough; and other and smaller fires blaze briskly all around within the rising wall—a fire on every mortarboard, which keeps the mortar plastic and the blood of the bricklayer uncongealed. Thus is the smitten city rising again at New Year's—rising, as she fell, by fire [Plate 67].

The number of brick and stone buildings in process of erection on the first day of December, on each street in the South Division, was as follows:

River Street	8	Polk Street	1
South Water Street	12	Michigan Avenue	3
Lake Street	10	Wabash Avenue	17
Randolph Street	6	State Street	24
Washington Street	6	Dearborn Street	6
Madison Street	29	Clark Street	16
Monroe Street	26	La Salle Street	4
Adams Street	2	Fifth Avenue	6
Quincy Street	1	Franklin Street	9
Jackson Street	1	Market Street	3
Van Buren Street	1	Miscellaneous	21
Harrison Street	2	Total	214

It is probable that a thousand stone and brick buildings will be in process of erection by May.

After the fire the Board of Public Works issued one-year permits for wooden buildings, which virtually abrogated the ordinance forbidding them within prescribed limits. In four weeks thereafter the North Side was covered with wooden buildings so thickly that it was difficult to see across the blocks, and a row of similar structures in the South Division soon stretched along the hitherto unoccupied park, on the east side of Michigan Avenue, a mile and a half, from the river's mouth to Twelfth Street. Two stories only were allowed, but some became very capacious warehouses, adapted to the largest demands of a wholesale traffic.

The gravest peril of the city now lies in the prolonged existence and ceaseless multiplication of these combustible piles of lumber. Fire limits were prescribed by a timid Common Council in the hour of its dissolution, but the ordinance is openly violated in every part of the city with perfect impunity. The first man has yet to be arrested or annoyed for furnishing food for the next great conflagration. It would seem that Chicago could scarcely afford an encore of the performance of October 8 and 9; but a repetition of that tragedy is just as certain to follow the persistence in our clapboard and shingle madness as is any given effect to succeed an adequate cause.

There is scarcely any city on the continent so exposed to prolonged and terrible winds as Chicago. Our constant imminent menace is that autumnal southwest hurricane which sweeps up from the wide prairie to the lake, eager to seize upon a spark and nurse it into a conflagration. Let a block get well on fire towards the Stock Yards in some densely settled locality, in the face of such a gale, and all the apparatus of the fire department must prove futile. Nothing but acres of solid brick, or stone buildings that are virtually fireproof can stop it.

A Chicago Directory

[From the *Chicago Evening Journal,* Tuesday, October 10, 1871.]

The following is a directory as far as we are able to make it out at this writing:

Chicago Evening Journal, 15 and 17 South Canal Street.

Board of Trade, 51 and 53 South Canal Street.

Post-office, Burlington Hall, corner Sixteenth Street.

Western Union Telegraph Company, Burlington Hall, corner of State and Sixteenth streets.

Common Council, new Congregational Church, corner of West Washington and Ann streets.

Board of Public Works, Masonic Building, corner West Randolph and Halsted streets.

The officers of the Illinois Central, and Chicago, Burlington and Quincy Railroads will be found at the ruins of their old depots. Their vaults are in great danger.

The U.S. Custom-house, U.S. Depository, Marshal's Courts, U.S. Commissioner Hoyne, will be located in the old Congregational Church, corner of Green and Washington.

The office for arrival and departure of vessels, at Light-house.

The *Tribune* office is in the same building as the *Journal*.

United States Pension office, rear of a drug store, corner of State and Sixteenth streets. The address of the agent, D. Blakely, is Michigan Avenue, 581.

Merchants' Saving Loan & Trust Company can be found at the residence of the President, Mr. S. A. Smith, 414 Wabash Avenue.

The proprietors of the Sherman House have bought P. W. Gates' Hotel, corner of Clinton and Madison streets, and will open immediately.

The Matteson House proprietors can be found at 579 West Washington Street, where all business will be transacted.

The Tremont House proprietors have purchased the Michigan Avenue Hotel, where they are now stationed.